AUDACIOUS

AUDACIOUS

A Bold Guide to Building the Life and Career You Want and Deserve

Marty McDonald

NASHVILLE—NEW YORK

Copyright © 2025 by Marty McDonald

Jacket design by Micah Kandros

Jacket copyright © 2025 by Hachette Book Group, Inc.

Hachette Book Group supports the right to free expression and the value of copyright. The purpose of copyright is to encourage writers and artists to produce the creative works that enrich our culture.

The scanning, uploading, and distribution of this book without permission is a theft of the author's intellectual property. If you would like permission to use material from the book (other than for review purposes), please contact permissions@hbgusa.com. Thank you for your support of the author's rights.

Worthy Books
Hachette Book Group
1290 Avenue of the Americas, New York, NY 10104
worthypublishing.com
X.com/WorthyPub

First Edition: October 2025

Worthy Books is a division of Hachette Book Group, Inc. The Worthy Books name and logo are trademarks of Hachette Book Group, Inc.

The publisher is not responsible for websites (or their content) that are not owned by the publisher.

The Hachette Speakers Bureau provides a wide range of authors for speaking events. To find out more, go to hachettespeakersbureau.com or email HachetteSpeakers@hbgusa.com.

Print book interior design by Marie Mundaca

Library of Congress Control Number: 2025940292

ISBN: 9781546009405 (Hardcover)

ISBN: 9781546009429 (E-Book)

ISBN: 9781668652565 (Downloadable Audio)

Printed in the United States of America

LSC-C

Printing 1, 2025

*To Kevin, Elle, Laila, and Ryan—
it's all possible if you simply believe*

Contents

Preface .... *ix*
Introduction .... *xiii*

CHAPTER 1: What the F? 1

CHAPTER 2: The Magic of Vision 23

CHAPTER 3: Flip the Script and Rewrite Your Story 41

CHAPTER 4: The Comparison Trap 51

CHAPTER 5: Shifting from Scarcity to Abundance 61

CHAPTER 6: The Audacity of Authenticity 77

CHAPTER 7: Stay True to Your "Why," Even When
It's Hard 93

Contents

CHAPTER 8: Ignite Your Connections 109

CHAPTER 9: Finding Your Voice: How to Craft an Audacious Pitch 133

CHAPTER 10: "No" Starts the Convo 149

CHAPTER 11: The ROI of Investing in Yourself 161

CHAPTER 12: The Real Secret Sauce Is Surrender 179

Conclusion 201
Acknowledgments 203
About the Author 205

Preface

AUDACIOUS: A BOLD GUIDE to Building the Life and Career You Want and Deserve is not just a book—it's a manifesto for anyone who's ready to stop playing it safe and start creating a life that's truly their own. Entrepreneur and trailblazer Marty McDonald takes readers on an unforgettable journey of risk, resilience, and transformation.

With unflinching honesty, McDonald recounts her personal stories of triumph and failure, offering an intimate look into the audacious decisions that propelled her from uncertainty to success. From navigating the unknown to breaking through barriers that seemed insurmountable, McDonald reveals the mindset, strategies, and bold actions required to turn fear into fuel and transform dreams into reality.

Through riveting anecdotes and hard-earned wisdom, *Audacious* dives deep into the pivotal moments when the stakes are highest—and when the choice to push forward can change everything. This book is not about playing it safe or following

Preface

the prescribed path. It's about stepping outside your comfort zone, seizing opportunities, and making decisions that will shape the future you truly deserve.

Whether you're looking to level up in your career, create a life of meaning, or embrace the wild unknown of new possibilities, *Audacious* provides the blueprint for creating a life filled with purpose, passion, and undeniable success. It's time to be fearless. It's time to be audacious.

This is the call to action you've been waiting for. Are you ready to get audacious?

AUDACIOUS

Introduction

IT WASN'T UNTIL I was thirty-two years old that I decided to bet on myself and finally walk into audacity. You know, the kind of audacity that makes folks whisper, *Who does she think she is? How could she ever do it?* Or, *Wow, she really believed in herself.*

I had just quit my corporate job. I remember the day I quit so vividly: I went into the office of my chief marketing officer and told her I would be putting in my two weeks' notice. The look on her face will always be ingrained in my memory as she asked, "What are you going to do?" That question was and still is my motivation. I can't get over how she believed so little in me. My response was: "Live my best life." In the back of my mind, I knew I could always come back and get a job because I was a trained and skilled professional, but I knew it was time to fly. As brave as I was in this moment, it was only preparation for the audacious day that would truly allow me to soar.

Four months after walking away from my corporate gig, I found myself on a flight to Los Angeles, heading to a women's

Introduction

entrepreneur conference. It was a make-or-break time in my journey—a time when hunger, determination, and a fierce desire to win consumed me. I knew I needed to be in a room filled with women who weren't just dreaming, but actively achieving, radiating the kind of energy that can only come from breaking barriers. That energy—their energy—was something I craved to ignite my own fire.

I wasn't alone. A fellow entrepreneur joined me, a kindred spirit equally obsessed with building something bigger. Day one of the conference was all about networking and finding your tribe, and day two was centered around breakouts and learning the hottest trends in the marketplace. When it was time to go to the different breakout sessions, I attended a panel about influencers trending on social media. The women on this panel were all celebrity influencers except one, who was the CEO of a high-end confectionery brand. She spoke about creating taboo gummy bears, like a green juice gummy or a whiskey-infused gummy, a launch they had recently produced, and the positive results that had come from it.

As she was speaking, something spoke to my soul. This idea wouldn't leave my spirit: *Marty, go up to her after this panel and pitch to her the data you recently saw on the power of Black women consumers. Ask her what "Black Girl Magic" is and if Black women are a part of her target audience.*

Whoa! Where did that thought come from? God, are you whispering to me? I wondered.

Hey, I thought, *what do I have to lose? I'm here in LA, and I'm ready to shake stuff up.*

You'll soon discover that I'm the type who pauses in storytelling, so let's pause here for a moment. I need to share a few details because this story holds the key to a game-changing lesson. Picture this: On the panel were big-name influencers, the kind everyone flocks to for a quick photo op. But I didn't waste my time chasing a picture for social media. Instead, I approached the woman who wasn't being chased by the crowd—the one who held the real power in the room.

I had something that this woman needed—revenue. I knew my idea would add a new customer segment that she was reaching for. But I needed something from her too: exposure, reach, and visibility to take my brand to the next level. I had quit my job with no savings. I had no fallback plan.

So, I went up to her and said, "Hey, Susan, I am Marty McDonald, CEO of Boss Women Media—a community created to gather women and share the most dynamic stories in the form of experiential storytelling for women's voices. Do you know what Black Girl Magic is?" I didn't give her time to answer before I shared my insight: "It is a rallying call for women to come together and unite. There is so much power in that, and you are missing out! Do you have Black women as a secondary target audience? You should let me create a gummy bear called Black Girl Magic, and I will bring my community to your stores to connect, gather, and purchase this product through a five-city tour called Black Girl Magic."

Let me pause and say this conversation only happened because I was intentional, fearless, and had a whole lot of audacity. I was scared but confident, and my pitch felt like a win-win for both parties.

I finally paused to see her response. I could see I had definitely piqued her curiosity, and she gave me an email address to send my pitch to her. Part of me wondered if she'd given me

Introduction

her junk mail address, but I didn't care. I had more than what I started with, and I was determined to send her the pitch that would not only change her business, but my business as well.

This was the moment when I first tapped into the power of being audacious. I had nothing to lose, and I needed to gain so much. I needed this to be my time to win. My audacity was my anchoring power! When I got on the plane back to Dallas, I was leaving Los Angeles no longer just hungry—I was leaving unstoppable. I whipped out my laptop and began dreaming, drafting, and creating the pitch deck that told the story of Boss Women Media. I created slides about women gathering. I touched on my reach, the impact that could be made, and how I would pack her stores with women of all backgrounds—influencers, celebrities, working women, and, ultimately, customers.

Six weeks later, Susan responded, and I was on a call pitching her a five-city tour and an opportunity to create a gummy bear called Black Girl Magic! An audacious thought that quickly turned itself into a pitch changed everything about my business and career trajectory—and it can do that for you too.

What Does Audacious *Really* Mean? And Why It Matters

Now, audacious is not a word we often use, so let me define what I mean by it. Audacious is being bold, not settling for "safe," and embracing the excitement and fear that come with courageously pursuing your true passions. It's about authentically believing that you deserve to live a life that truly excites you.

Audacity is not just a word—it's a mindset, a daily practice, and the catalyst for solving the world's problems, reshaping ecosystems, and living a life of fulfillment. For the past eight years, I have embraced audacity every single day in both my

Introduction

business and personal life. It has been my secret sauce to breaking free from mediocrity. And now, I stand in this moment with you—to pass the torch and show you what's possible.

> Audacious is being bold, not settling for "safe," and embracing the excitement and fear that come with courageously pursuing your true passions.

The Heart of Audacious: Why This Book Exists

This book tackles a fundamental problem so many of us face: playing it safe. We've been taught that the "safe" path is the right path—the one that leads to security and stability. But in reality, playing it safe often gets you a safe life filled with limited opportunities, muted joy, and unrealized potential. Safe is not fulfilling. Safe is not what you were created for. It's a mindset that keeps you small, confined, and far from the richness of life you are meant to experience.

I chose the word *audacious* as the title of this book because it represents the exact shift we need to make. Audaciousness isn't just about being fearless—it's about stepping boldly and unapologetically into a life of abundance, authority, and purpose. It's about recognizing that you were created to live a life that is not just "safe," but rich, full, and transformative.

When you shift your mindset from playing small to stepping into audacity, everything changes. Audacity leads to the kind of life where opportunities multiply, where you walk in authority and possibility, and where you start creating a lasting legacy. It's not just about having the courage to dream big—it's about taking the bold, intentional actions that make those dreams a reality.

Introduction

Audacity empowers you to push beyond your limits, take meaningful risks, and create a life rooted in curiosity, possibility, and happiness. When you anchor your actions in audacity, you don't just live differently—you inspire innovation, challenge outdated systems, and drive transformation in workplaces, communities, and the world at large.

> **Audaciousness isn't just about being fearless—it's about stepping boldly and unapologetically into a life of abundance, authority, and purpose.**

Here's the reality: Staying on the sidelines, hesitating, or wavering only feeds the fears that whisper, "You can't. You never will. You're not enough." But those fears are liars. Audacity silences them. It's the vehicle that empowers you to show up boldly and unapologetically, breaking through barriers to live the life of your dreams.

Why the World Needs Audacious People (and You Owe It to Yourself)

We owe it to ourselves—and to the legacy of our ancestors—to live boldly. We are walking in their wildest dreams. The least we can carry from their sacrifices is the audacity to live a life that isn't flat, but full, prosperous, and whole.

But let's take a second to address the elephant in the room: Audacity has long been viewed negatively, often associated with arrogance or overstepping. But today, we're reclaiming it. Audacity isn't about disrespect—it's about boldness, authority, and the courage to make positive, meaningful change. It's about saying "yes" to dreaming bigger, challenging the status quo, and stepping fully into the life you're meant to lead.

Introduction

For too long, we've been conditioned to ask for permission—to play by rules that stifle our creativity and joy. I was tired of that life. Maybe you are too. The truth is, no one is coming to save us. If you want to walk in authority, live greatly, and disrupt the status quo, you must embrace audacity. It is the cure for an unfulfilled life. It's not enough to simply avoid fear; we must take authority over our lives and embody a mindset of radical possibility and joy.

Audacity is the answer to the problem of mediocrity. It is the authority you need to own your space, drive change, and live greatly. The world needs your boldness. Step into it. Every single day.

More than Just Dreams: The Key to Unlocking Your Potential

This book isn't just about dreaming big—it's about giving you the practical tools to embrace boldness, courage, and authenticity, and to master the blueprint for living audaciously. Whether you're a business owner, a leader, or someone ready to take charge of your life, this book will guide you to remove fears, carry a vision, craft your story, shift your mindset, unlock your network, leave space for miracles, and elevate your life or business to the next level.

Being audacious isn't just a concept—it's a foolproof way of living the life you desire. Through this book, you'll not only dream bigger but also define your vision, lean into the risks, and embrace the good, the bad, and the ugly that come along the journey of bold living. Audacity is the key to breaking barriers, creating opportunities, and turning your wildest dreams into reality.

Introduction

We'll walk through my personal audacious stories of winning, losing, and learning. You'll see the behind-the-scenes truth of my ambitious journey—one where I refused to settle for anything less than my dreams. From being broke, hungry, and misunderstood to building a life anchored in audacity, I share how these experiences shaped me and how you can use the lessons I've learned to identify your own dreams, values, and goals—and most importantly, align your actions to achieve them.

This book will also challenge the story you've been telling yourself. Is it one of victory and possibility, or one filled with doubt and fear? Together, we'll rewrite that story. You'll learn how to win and intentionally create the life of your dreams.

My Audacious Journey: From Then to Now

I know firsthand how transformative an audacious mindset can be. You see, I come from a single-parent household in a small town in Tennessee. A place where last names matter, and if you grow up on the wrong side of the tracks, that train could dictate your future. I was born in the '80s, grew up in the '90s, and was one of the first biracial kids in my town. Identity has been something I have wrestled with for a long time, and I grew some pretty thick skin to endure kids taunting me, grown-ups placing me in a box I wasn't sure how to check, and having no resources to help on either side.

Can I tell you, though, that God is so real, because even though I did not have my dad's last name, did not grow up in the "right" neighborhood, and definitely did not see what a working parent looked like, I knew my story would be insanely different from my circumstances. Why?

Introduction

Because ever since I could remember I wanted MORE!
I was brave!
Beyond curious!

And I knew that more existed because I exposed myself to different ways of living through the lives of my friends and all that they had. I knew life could be grand if I dug deep and clawed through to get out of my small town.

I made my way into corporate America and thrived, but quickly realized that while I was breaking barriers with my own trajectory, I was also alone and isolated. In the last three companies where I had worked, I was the only Black woman on the marketing teams and sometimes the only Black person at the company. The sense of being the only one left me feeling alone and isolated. I wrestled with imposter syndrome daily: Should I be here? Do I belong? After all, I didn't come from the same cultural background as most of my white colleagues! When we don't see anyone who looks like us in positions and places we desire to be in, it's easy to begin losing hope of what's possible. And when you don't see what's possible, in many ways, it does not exist.

I was a first-generation college graduate, so I had no example of anyone working in corporate America. When it came to my career and future, I was told to play it safe and be happy that I'd made it this far. The rebel in me couldn't shake the idea of more, though. I was excited by the possibility that I could create something I was passionate about—and experience financial freedom in the process, although I had no idea what financial freedom even looked like for me and my family at that time. But the idea of more, and of the financial freedom that would come with more, was my anchor.

Introduction

Audacity isn't just something I talk about—it's how I've lived my life and built my success, brick by bold brick. My journey began with humble origins, navigating challenges that many of us know all too well—being broke, being hungry, being left out, and being misunderstood. Yet through it all, I refused to let any of those circumstances define or limit me. Instead, I made audacity my anchor, the driving force that propelled me forward.

I knew there had to be a group of other audacious women who desired more, and I needed to surround myself with these women. In 2016, even before I quit my corporate job, I gathered twenty-five women together for a brunch to talk about balance, dreams, and careers. Later, I started my vision by hosting a gathering with a small group of twenty audacious women, and those humble beginnings grew into what would later become the foundation for the company I built: Boss Women Media. Today, as the CEO of Boss Women Media, I lead a company that empowers and inspires over one hundred thousand audacious women across the country. Through transformative events, workshops, and community-building initiatives, we equip women with the tools and confidence to own their power, shatter glass ceilings, and rewrite their stories. What was once only a vision is now a movement.

But my audacious journey didn't stop there. In 2022, I took another bold leap and launched Elle Olivia, a children's lifestyle brand designed to empower Black girls up to age five. Available in over four hundred Target locations nationwide, this line celebrates representation, joy, and the belief that even the youngest among us can dream big and live boldly.

Introduction

What took me from my humble beginnings to corporate queen and NOW high-powered CEO, media mogul, and fashion designer? The power of audacity. It's the same mindset that allowed me to leave the safety of a corporate career to build something that didn't just reflect my dreams but also impacted the lives of so many others.

Why am I the expert to guide you on this journey? Because I've walked this path. I've faced the fear of failure, the pain of rejection, and the temptation to settle. I didn't allow the struggles or setbacks to define or deter me. Every time, I chose audacity. It's been the secret ingredient to my success, and now I'm here to share it with you.

> **Audacity isn't something you're born with—it's something you learn.**

If I Can, You Can Too

In this book, I'll take you behind the scenes of my journey—the wins, the losses, and the lessons that shaped me. Together, we'll explore how audacity can shift your mindset, unlock your potential, and elevate your life or business to the next level. If I can create a life of abundance, authority, and impact by embracing audacity, so can you.

Because here's the truth: Audacity isn't something you're born with—it's something you learn. And it works for anyone who's willing to apply it.

Let me tell you about April. If there was someone who was the antithesis of audacious, it was her. When I first met April, she was stuck in a cycle of self-doubt and hesitation. She had big dreams of starting her own business but felt paralyzed by

Introduction

fear—fear of rejection, fear of failure, and fear of being seen as "too much." She played it safe in her corporate job, despite feeling unfulfilled and burned out.

Then, April attended one of my Boss Women Media events. For the first time, she was surrounded by a community of ambitious, audacious women who weren't afraid to disrupt the status quo. During one of the sessions, I shared my own story and the tools I used to step into my audacity, and something clicked for April. She realized she didn't have to wait for permission or perfection to take her first step.

April began applying the principles of audacity to her life. She leaned into the risks, created a bold vision for her business, and started taking small but consistent steps toward her dream. She attended networking events, pitched her ideas fearlessly, and launched her business within six months. Today, April's company is thriving, she's earning more than she ever did in her corporate job, and she's inspiring others with her journey.

In the end, April's audacity propelled her to greater heights, and the same can be true for you.

Now is your time. Not tomorrow. Not next year. Right now. This is the moment to step into the boldness that's been calling you—to stop playing it safe and start living the life you're meant to live. Let me be clear: Waiting to embrace audacity is choosing to stay stuck. Every moment you hesitate is a moment lost—an opportunity left on the table, a dream deferred, a life not fully lived. You don't have to wait for the perfect time to start because there's no such thing. Right now is the right time. You were led to pick up this book for a reason. *Audacious*

> **Waiting to embrace audacity is choosing to stay stuck.**

Introduction

is not just a collection of stories or ideas; it's your personal blueprint for transformation. Get ready to experience the most incredible transformation and the exhilarating joy that comes with stepping into your boldest, most audacious self.

What This Book Will Do for You

Here's why this book will change your life for the better:

1. **Audacity is one of the most important traits of successful people.**
   If you look at anyone who's made a significant impact—whether in their personal life, career, or community—you'll find one thing in common: audacity. It's the ability to say yes to risks, to believe in possibilities that others don't see, and to push forward even when fear looms large.
2. **Audacity makes you less afraid to take risks.**
   Fear is the biggest roadblock to the life you want. But when you embrace audacity, fear loses its grip. You'll learn how to reframe risks, step outside your comfort zone, and make bold moves with confidence, knowing that even setbacks are part of the process.
3. **Audacity helps you overcome being told "no" in life, which ultimately results in more "yes."**
   Life is full of rejection—it's unavoidable. But audacity gives you the power to persist, to pivot, and to keep going until the "no" becomes a "yes." When you stop taking rejection personally and start using it as fuel, you'll open doors you never thought possible.

4. **Audacity makes you more resilient.**
   The road to success isn't easy, but audacity strengthens your ability to endure challenges and setbacks. It teaches you to adapt, to bounce back, and to keep moving forward with an unshakable belief in yourself and your vision.

This book will teach you how to harness the power of audacity to shift your mindset, take bold action, and create a life of purpose, passion, and success. You'll learn how to identify your dreams, align your actions, and carry the vision for your life and career to the next level.

This book is structured around twelve principles of audacity, with a dedicated chapter for each. These principles will help you master the blueprint for audacious living and give you actionable strategies for embracing boldness, courage, and authenticity.

Unlike some self-help books, *Audacious* isn't just about theory—it's packed with practical, proven tools to help you:

- Remove fears and limiting beliefs.
- Define your vision and align it with your values.
- Craft your unique story to inspire and connect with others.
- Shift your mindset to embrace boldness, courage, and authenticity.
- Unlock your network and create opportunities.
- Leave space for miracles while building a strategy for success.

Introduction

This book is your guide to rewriting the story you tell yourself and stepping into a life that's bigger, bolder, and more fulfilled than you've ever imagined. If you're ready to overcome fear, shatter limitations, and become the person you're meant to be, then *Audacious* is for you.

How to Use This Book

Think of this book as your mentor, your guide, or even a conversation with your boldest, most fearless friend. The chapters are designed to build on one another, so I recommend reading them in order. But this isn't a race—take your time to absorb each principle and put it to work. Practice one tool at a time, reflect on the lessons, and then move forward. Keep this book close and refer back to it whenever you need a push to keep stepping into your audacity.

Every story, every lesson, every tool is designed to get you ready to transform everything—from your mindset to your future. You'll learn to conquer fear, cast a powerful vision, craft your own unique story, shift your mentality, activate your network, and open yourself up to amazing possibilities in your life and career.

Buckle up! We're about to embark on a ride where I'll show you how to refuse to settle for anything less than your dreams—with audacity. Together, we'll unlock the blueprint for boldness, courage, and authenticity, transforming every aspect of your life and stepping into the extraordinary.

This isn't just about being ambitious; it's about being audacious. What's the difference? Being ambitious is the desire to do it. Being audacious is having the guts to actually do it! Audacity

Introduction

> **Being ambitious is the desire to do it. Being audacious is having the guts to actually do it!**

turns dreams into action, challenges into opportunities, and ordinary lives into extraordinary stories. Audacious isn't just a word—it's the key to everything you've been waiting for.

Let's rewrite your story together. Stick with me on this journey, soak up the lessons, and take bold action, and you will transform your life. Let's start your audacious journey now!

CHAPTER 1

What the F?

"WHAT THE F?" THE words ripped from my mouth before I could stop them. My hands shook as I stared at the invoice—the biggest bill of my life. My chest tightened, and a cold sweat broke out on my skin. How in the world was I supposed to handle this? My heart thundered like a drumbeat of panic, and my breath came in shallow, uneven gasps. You know that feeling, that raw, visceral moment when fear grabs hold of you and won't let go? My legs buckled beneath me, as if the weight of my terror was too much for them to bear. Every worst-case scenario flashed before my eyes.

Big fears—no, *monstrous* fears—engulfed me like a tidal wave, threatening to drown me in doubt and despair. The full story of what happened next unfolds in Chapter 7, but for now, just know that this was a *really* big bill, and I was *not* expecting it. I was afraid.

We've all been there—gripped by fear, feeling it deep in our bones, and maybe you're even walking through a season of it right now. Fear can feel paralyzing because it thrives when we feel out of control. How many of us have faced moments when we couldn't control the outcome—a deal that fell through, a bill you don't have the money to pay for, a promotion that slipped away, the unpredictable challenges of parenting, pregnancy, marriage, and so much more? We've all been there, caught in the grip of uncertainty, unsure of what will happen next.

I'm convinced fear is the greatest obstacle to living an audacious life and building the life and career you deserve. It's so pivotal that I decided we must slay this enemy to audacity right from the start of this book. In this chapter, we'll delve into the nature of fear. We will explore the intricate relationship between fear and audacity, understand how it holds us back, and, most importantly, discover how to transform fear into the very fuel that propels us toward audacious action. So let's talk about the F word. Fear.

> **Fear is the greatest obstacle to living an audacious life and building the life and career you deserve.**

The Fear That Shaped My Journey

Fear has been a constant shadow in my life. My childhood threw me into situations that constantly felt overwhelming and terrifying. Although I always found a way through, learning how to navigate and overcome fear took time. And even today, in writing about this subject, I'm choosing to set aside my fear of being judged so I can share with you the most intimate parts of my journey—how fear showed up in one of the most unexpected places, my desire to grow my family—and how I faced that fear and found my way through.

What the F?

It started in 2017, when after seven years of marriage, my husband and I decided it was time to expand our family. All around us, friends were getting pregnant, so we didn't even consider the possibility that it wouldn't happen for us. When we tried for the first time, I was eager—so eager, in fact, that I took a pregnancy test when I was just four weeks along. To my delight, it was positive. I was thrilled! I could finally say, "I'm pregnant, just like everyone else."

It's funny how we often get caught up in *monkey see, monkey do*. We follow the paths of those around us, believing that if everyone else is doing it, it must be right. I was caught up in that same mindset, convinced that getting pregnant and becoming a mom was the next step I was supposed to take, just like all my friends. Looking back now, I wonder how much we miss out on when we imitate others instead of embracing our own unique journey. This was my first lesson.

As I thought about the future, I began preparing myself for the changes that would come with a growing belly. The first thing I did? Binge eat. I vividly remember indulging in a ten-piece order of flats from Wingstop with extra crispy, extra saucy mild and parmesan wings—and, of course, ranch dipping sauce. It was as if I was already preparing for my "pregnant body."

But just three days into my pregnancy, my excitement was cut short. I woke up to unexpected bleeding. It was my first miscarriage. The rush of disbelief, confusion, and heartbreak was overwhelming. I felt empty, scared, and ashamed. I couldn't understand why it happened. All I could think was, *Everyone else is getting pregnant. Why not me?*

Looking back, I'm not sure if I wanted to be pregnant as much as I wanted to be *like everyone else*. I had let the news of other people expanding their families become a benchmark for my own life, a measure of where I should be. It's a trap we all fall into—**comparing** our lives to others—and it makes us lose sight of our own path. I found myself questioning everything, wondering if I had done something wrong. But fear of the unknown and comparison only made the pain harder to process.

Here's something I found to be true—the biggest fears tend to surface when you're in alignment with your true path, and they can overwhelm you the moment you start comparing your journey to others.

Months passed, and though I was still grieving, my husband and I decided to try again. Trying again wasn't easy, though. I had to reconnect with my "why"—the real reason I wanted a family. It wasn't about being like everyone else; it was about us, our future, and the family we wanted to build. I had to refocus on what truly mattered to me, not the timeline or expectations set by others.

But even after that, we faced more heartache. The second miscarriage came a few months later, and this time, I had to undergo a D&C because I was too far along for the pregnancy to pass naturally. The fear and isolation that followed were intense. I felt lost, wondering what was wrong with me and blaming myself for both miscarriages.

When things don't go as we hope, it's easy to fall into a spiral of self-blame. We convince ourselves we did something wrong. We question our worth. But this book isn't about staying stuck in those fears. It's about rewriting the narrative and using those fears as fuel for growth, strength, and success.

During those painful times, I couldn't help but think about what others might be saying. I imagined whispers and judgment. *Why is it taking her so long? What's wrong with her?* It's easy to let our **insecurities** creep in, especially when we're hurting. But if you're going through grief—whether it's from a miscarriage, a job loss, or a failed relationship—don't let the noise of others' opinions drown out your healing process. Protect your peace. Keep your story to yourself while you heal.

Another fear I wrestled with was judgment. I feared what people would think of me, my struggles, and my inability to have a baby when others seemed to have it so easy. But I learned something important: If people truly care about you, they won't judge you for your setbacks. They'll uplift and support you. Judgment often comes from past traumas or insecurities that others haven't healed from.

The fear of **isolation** hit me hard. I didn't have what all my friends had—the pregnancy announcements, the celebrations, the joy. I felt alone in a world where everyone else seemed so connected. As a woman, there's a pressure to be strong, to nurture others, and to maintain composure even when you're falling apart. It's hard to admit when you feel alone, especially when society expects you to be the one holding it all together.

For me, this fear wasn't just about physical isolation; it was emotional loneliness. The feeling that no one understood my pain, my struggles, or what I was going through. I put on a brave face, as we often do, pretending everything was fine even when I felt like I was falling apart inside.

But over time, I've learned that it's okay to reach out, to be vulnerable, and to ask for help. I've started to create space for myself to process my emotions—whether that's through journaling, taking long walks, or simply sitting with my feelings. It's still a journey, but I'm learning that acknowledging my loneliness, rather than hiding it, is the first step in overcoming it.

Another fear that haunted me during this time was the **fear of the future**. What if we tried again and failed again? What if it never happened? The fear of future loss can be paralyzing, especially when past disappointments linger. But I realized that setbacks don't define our entire journey. By reflecting on the strength I gained through those challenges, I was able to shift my perspective and embrace hope again.

The key to overcoming that fear of the future was focusing on small victories, learning from the past, and trusting that the right time would come. By holding on to hope and shifting my mindset, I was able to turn fear into a source of strength, not limitation.

Maybe you can relate to some of these fears—not necessarily through pregnancy, but through other life challenges. Whether it's finding love, standing up for yourself at work, or taking that leap to pursue your dreams, fear is real. It's thick, heavy, and paralyzing. But on the other side of fear is opportunity, growth, and joy. I'm living proof of that.

After the second miscarriage, my husband and I decided to wait about a year and a half before trying again. During that time, I focused on my own healing, both physically and emotionally. I leaned on my faith and asked others to pray for me—not just to get pregnant, but to stay pregnant. When I think back on the timing, I realize how perfectly everything worked out. If I had gotten pregnant right away in 2017, I would have been overwhelmed with responsibilities and may never have taken the leap to leave my job. I would have missed opportunities to meet people like Susan, who played a key role in my journey. Timing is everything. There is a time for everything, and sometimes your goals and desires are meant to unfold in their own perfect timing.

> The biggest fears tend to surface when you're in alignment with your true path, and they can overwhelm you the moment you start comparing your journey to others.

The Fear-Audacity Paradox

Here's the paradox: Fear and audacity are two sides of the same coin. The same fear that seeks to paralyze you is the very thing that audacity rises above. When you feel that knot in your stomach, that voice whispering, "You can't do this," it's the moment you must push forward. Because being audacious is not the absence of fear—it's the decision to act in spite of it.

Fear is a natural response to stepping into the unknown. It's the body's way of trying to protect you, of keeping you safe within the familiar, the predictable. It's as old as human survival instincts: Don't take risks. Don't wander too far from the herd. Stay safe. And yet, to live an audacious life—the kind where you step into your power, take risks, and achieve your dreams—you must do the opposite. You must move through fear.

The relationship between fear and audacity is complex. Fear often arises when you are on the verge of a breakthrough, when you're about to step into something bigger than yourself. And audacity? It's the courage that fights back. It's the voice that says, "Yes, I'm scared, but I'm going to do it anyway." It's the choice to move forward with boldness, to keep walking even when the road ahead is uncertain.

The Grip of Fear: How It Manifests

> The same fear that seeks to paralyze you is the very thing that audacity rises above.

Everyone feels fear—it's a natural part of being human. Think of fear like a built-in warning system. It's there to protect us from real danger. But in today's world, that alarm often goes off even when there's no actual fire—it's just a false alarm based on our worries. Common fear-based mindsets that can hinder audacity include fear of failure, fear of judgment, fear of the future, and fear of the unknown. These are the big ones. Maybe you've experienced them all, or maybe one of them has paralyzed you at some point in your life.

- **Fear of failure** makes you question whether you're capable or worthy.
- **Fear of judgment** makes you wonder if others will criticize, reject, or laugh at you.
- **Fear of the future** keeps you stuck in the "what ifs"—what if things don't work out? What if I'm not prepared for what's next?
- **Fear of the unknown** can keep you in a constant state of indecision, unsure of which direction to take.

This list of fears is not exhaustive by any means. Fear can also manifest in other ways that are harder to spot:

- **Procrastination:** Have you ever found yourself putting off that big decision or that challenging task, telling yourself "I'll do it later"? That's fear, dressed up as procrastination.

- **Self-doubt:** When you're consumed by self-doubt, you question your worth and abilities, even though you know you have what it takes. That's fear playing tricks on your mind.
- **Avoidance:** This is when you avoid stepping into your true potential because the unknown seems too daunting.
- **Analysis paralysis:** Overthinking every detail can prevent you from taking any action at all.
- **Imposter Syndrome** is the feeling of being a fraud, despite evidence of your competence and success.
- **Perfectionism**, or the fear of not being good enough, can cause you to avoid taking risks or stepping out of your comfort zone.

Identifying your specific fears and the mentalities that perpetuate them is crucial for moving forward.

The most dangerous thing about fear is how it holds us back. It keeps us from reaching our full potential, from living the audacious lives we deserve. Fear can leave us stuck in a cycle of **comparison**, constantly measuring ourselves against others and feeling like we're not enough. It feeds **insecurity** and fosters a sense of **isolation**. It makes us believe we are alone in our struggles, disconnected from those who could support us, and far from the life we long to create.

But here's the truth: Fear is not the enemy. Fear is simply a signal. It's an emotion that stems from our past experiences, our traumas, and our unresolved doubts. In many cases, fear is rooted in past pain—moments in our lives where we felt rejected, abandoned, or unworthy. That's why it feels so intense.

Audacious

It taps into the things we've yet to heal or address. But what if we reframed our relationship with fear?

For example, think of the first time you tried something completely out of your comfort zone. Whether it was a business venture, a creative project, or an important conversation, fear tried to stop you. But your audacity—the sheer act of doing it despite the fear—allowed you to experience growth. It didn't erase the fear; it simply put it in its place.

Instead of seeing fear as a roadblock, what if we saw it as a catalyst for growth? Fear can either keep us stuck in our comfort zone or push us to step into the unknown and grow. The decision is ours. Fear doesn't have to be a barrier; it can be the very thing that propels us forward. It can show us exactly where we need to grow, where we need to heal, and where we need to trust ourselves.

> **Fear is not the enemy.**
> **Fear is simply a signal.**

From Fear to Audacity: Shifting Your Mindset

The first step to living an audacious life is choosing to face your fears. Fear is inevitable. It will test you over and over again. But the question is: Will you let it control you, or will you control it? I've found some strategies that work practically for overcoming fear. These are the keys I use day in and day out in my life and that have led me to a life of audacious success. Here's my foolproof action plan to shift from a fear-based mindset to an audacious one.

Change the Story You Tell Yourself

The story you tell yourself is the blueprint for your life. If you tell yourself that you can't, then you won't. But if you start telling yourself that you can, that you're worthy, and that you are more than capable, you'll begin to move into alignment with that belief. Your actions will follow your mindset, doors will open where you once saw walls, and the life you once dreamed of will start to take shape before your eyes.

1. **Realize That Fear Is Just a Signal of Growth and Reframe It.**
   When you feel afraid, let that be a sign that you're on the verge of something significant, something that truly matters to you. Acknowledge your fear, then reframe the narrative: Say, "I am capable. I can handle challenges. Fear is a stepping stone, not a roadblock."
2. **Unleash Boldness, Courage, and Faith.**
   Boldness is the antidote to fear. Every time you feel fear creeping in, choose boldness. Trust in your abilities and the journey ahead. Courage isn't the absence of fear; it's the ability to act despite it. Lean into your faith—not just in the divine but in your own power to rise above.
3. **Embrace a Mindset of Persistence.**
   Audacity doesn't come from a single courageous act—it's a mentality built over time. Persistence is key. Every "no" is an opportunity to learn. Every setback is a lesson in resilience. Keep pushing forward, even when the road gets tough.
4. **Break Large Goals down into Manageable Tasks.**
   Fear often feels overwhelming when the goal seems too big. But the more you break things down into smaller, more manageable tasks, the less scary the

process becomes. Take the first step. Then the next. Soon, you'll realize that the seemingly impossible is actually achievable.

5. **Prioritize Self-Belief and Silence Societal Expectations.**
Society loves to tell us who we should be and what we should have, but none of that matters if it doesn't align with your truth. Prioritize your own self-belief over the opinions of others. The world will try to fit you into boxes, but audacity comes from stepping outside them and defining your own path.

6. **Understand That Small, Fearless Actions Compound over Time.**
The most transformative changes in your life don't happen overnight. They come from consistent, small actions that build momentum. Take small, fearless steps, and over time, those actions will lead to significant transformations. The key is to keep moving, even when progress feels slow.

Now, I wish I could tell you that once you master the strategies for overcoming fear, it will be like muscle memory and you'll be done with fear for good. But here's an important truth you must know about fear... Fear doesn't just disappear once you've faced one major challenge. Fear will try to test you again and again. It's not a one-and-done experience. And if anything, it gets bigger, scarier, and more complex. Fear certainly raised its ugly head in my life again, but this time, the outcome was much different.

The Fear That Led to Freedom

It was 2020. The world came to a standstill—lockdowns, no events, no social gatherings, and even date nights with a couple friends were relegated to Zoom.

> **Fear can either keep us stuck in our comfort zone or push us to step into the unknown and grow.**

Everything we knew to be normal was turned upside down. And as if the world's uncertainty wasn't enough, I found myself in a personal battle, trying to conceive in the midst of a pandemic.

To say the timing was strange is an understatement. While the world seemed to be spiraling into isolation and chaos, I found myself craving stillness. As the COVID-19 pandemic forced the world to pause, it brought with it a strange sense of calm that I didn't realize I needed. It was as though the stillness—both externally and internally—was exactly the space I needed to allow life to grow inside me.

But let me be clear: Isolation doesn't always feel like a gift. At first, it felt suffocating. But in that stillness, I began to change the narrative I had been telling myself about motherhood, about pregnancy, and about what I could truly control. That, of course, is a lesson for another chapter, but it was through this unexpected solitude that I learned something important: Fear can either hold you back or be the very catalyst for growth.

Fear, in its most paralyzing form, often shows up when we don't feel in control. And in this case, the fear I carried from my previous miscarriages began to creep back into my mind. It wasn't just the fear of loss—it was the fear of rejection. The fear of it happening again, the heartbreak, the emptiness. I had experienced that before, and I didn't want to go through it anew.

But what I didn't realize at the time was that *fear* wasn't something to avoid or hide from. It was a signal. It was showing me exactly where I needed to grow. The question was: *Could I face it head-on and transform it?*

The first step was leaning into that fear. And when I really examined it, I realized why I was so afraid. It wasn't just the fear of loss—it was a deeper fear of rejection. Fear of not being enough, of hearing "no" and letting it define me. So many of us carry this same fear. How many times do we hold back from pursuing our dreams, not because the dreams are too big or impossible, but because we fear rejection? It's not the failure that paralyzes us, it's the thought of being judged, of not being accepted.

But I had to remind myself: Rejection isn't a reflection of my worth. It's a part of the journey. It's a lesson, a redirection, and sometimes, even a necessary pause before the right "yes" comes along.

I never quite got comfortable being pregnant. I mean, sure, I was excited, but every day was a battle with my own fears. I held my breath throughout the entire pregnancy. After all, how could I not? Every time fear crept in—every time the "what ifs" of rejection started to bubble up—I had to confront it, look it in the eye, and say, *Not today*. I had to rewrite the story in my head. This wasn't about avoiding fear; it was about moving through it.

When I was twenty-four weeks pregnant, we received some earth-shattering news. My daughter had a birth defect—a hernia so severe that her spleen, liver, and intestines were positioned in her chest, covering her lungs. The doctors told us she had a 50/50 chance of surviving. The only way to save her would be to perform major surgery immediately after she was born to reposition everything back where it belonged.

After already surviving two miscarriages, I now had to face this unimaginable fear. Every day felt heavy, like I was carrying the weight of the world. I remember constantly checking my mental list, doing whatever I could to keep myself grounded and focused, just to make it through another moment. I couldn't share this with anyone—not even our parents. Only four close friends knew the truth, and even that felt like too much to bear. The thought of telling anyone else and adding to their worry was just too much. Sometimes, we have to hold certain things close to our hearts—keeping them between ourselves, our God, and maybe a trusted therapist.

Those months were a blur of fear, uncertainty, and emotional exhaustion. But I knew I had no choice but to keep moving forward, even when it felt like I was holding my breath in the dark.

I delivered at thirty-seven weeks—full term—and our beautiful daughter went into surgery just three days after birth. The doctors worked tirelessly to place everything back where it belonged. We spent thirty-five days in the NICU while her lungs developed, and those days were some of the hardest of my life. But at the end of it all, we took our warrior baby home. She was healthy. She was strong. I had just delivered a miracle.

It felt like a dream, but it was also a new chapter—one filled with joy and profound relief. But more than that, it was a chapter of overcoming. I became a mother, yes, but I also became a version of myself I never knew I could be. I had faced my deepest fears and survived, and in doing so, I learned what true strength felt like. The fear had never disappeared, but I had learned to walk through it, and it had changed me.

This was more than just a lesson about fear; it was a story of what it looks like to confront fear head-on and push through it. It was a story of how fear can shape and deepen relationships—how it brought my husband and me closer together, and how it strengthened my connection to God. The fear was still there, but I no longer saw it as something that would hold me back. It had become a teacher, one that showed me my own resilience.

The year 2020 might have been one of fear for many, but it was also the year that I learned to turn that fear into fuel. It became my push to move forward, to keep going even when things felt uncertain. I had to learn that fear is not a roadblock; it's a signpost. It points to where I need to grow, and it challenges me to show up for my own life.

Maybe you can relate. Fear has always been there, hasn't it? That knot in your stomach, the racing thoughts—it never fully goes away. But maybe it's not supposed to. What if fear is just a reminder that you're stepping into something that truly matters? It's not there to stop you; it's there to show you that you're growing, stretching beyond what feels safe. I know it's hard, but being brave doesn't mean waiting for the fear to disappear—it means taking the next step *with* it, trusting that fear is proof you're on the right path. Let it be your guide, not your barrier.

> **Fear can either hold you back or be the very catalyst for growth.**

What the F?

The Fear That Transformed Me: A Journey of Strength and Growth

And here's where the story takes another unexpected turn. A year and a half after the birth of our daughter, I found myself pregnant again. But this time, it wasn't just one baby—there were *two*. Yep, you heard that right. I was pregnant with twins. A year of abundance, sure, but I was terrified.

I had just conquered the fear of losing my first child, of navigating a traumatic pregnancy, and now here I was, facing the unknown again. Twins? Double the joy, sure. But also double the fear. Double the possibility of something going wrong. My mind was racing with all the "what ifs."

The fear hit me like a ton of bricks when I found out I was expecting twins. I was already overwhelmed with one child, and the idea of being responsible for three little people? It made my stomach drop. How could I handle that? How could I be *enough*?

I've always been the type A personality—the "go-getter," the achiever, the one who thrives on control—as an Eight on the **Enneagram list of personality types**. Sidenote, for those not familiar: The Enneagram is basically a personality tool, but it's *so much more* than just finding out if you're an introvert or an extrovert.

And for me, I hated feeling out of control. I hated the idea that I might not be able to "win" in this new chapter of my life. I was scared of failing, scared of not being able to keep it all together. And if I'm being honest, I was also scared that I wouldn't be *enough* for these little ones.

You see, growing up, there were times when I didn't feel taken care of. I went to bed hungry more nights than I'd like to admit, and that experience carved a deep fear in me that I swore my children would never have to face. I was determined that they wouldn't know what it felt like to struggle in that way, and the thought of being overwhelmed by three kids—three precious lives that I'd have to care for—felt like too much. It triggered that deep, old wound inside of me, and I was terrified of repeating the cycle.

On top of that, I was winning in business. I had a thriving seven-figure company, and it was growing fast. I was reaching heights I'd only dreamed of, and the success was exhilarating. But now, with twins on the way, I couldn't help but think: *Would they hold me back?* Would having two more kids derail everything I had worked so hard for?

And let's not even talk about the NICU experience. I had already been through that terrible pain with my first child, and the thought of going through that again, the uncertainty, the helplessness—it was almost too much to bear.

But here's what I learned: **Fear is sneaky**. It creeps up in ways we don't always see coming. It can paralyze us, trapping us in patterns that feel impossible to break. I realized that the habits I had developed—habits of fear, worry, and perfectionism—were the very things holding me back from stepping into this new chapter with confidence. And I wasn't just scared of the unknown; I was also *stuck* in a cycle of repeating these old fears, over and over again.

These habits, these patterns of fear, had become so ingrained in me that they felt automatic. I had grown used to them. But I couldn't afford to let them control me anymore—not with the twins on the way, and not with the future I wanted to build.

So I decided to do something radical: I had to face my fears head-on. I had to stop letting fear dictate my life and start rewriting the story. Fear didn't get to have the final say anymore.

Fear didn't own me anymore. I was stronger, more prepared. Fear had become my companion, not my enemy. It was a muscle I had learned to flex, strengthen, and use to fuel my next big challenge. The fear didn't go away, but it no longer controlled me. I was now in control of how I responded to it.

And with that, I entered into the journey of carrying twins with a new mindset. The fear was still present, but it didn't paralyze me. It didn't stop me from celebrating the life growing inside me. Instead, it motivated me. It pushed me to prepare for the unexpected, to trust in the process, and to lean into faith even more deeply than I had before. And in the end, that trust, that faith, led me to the most beautiful moment of my life—the birth of my two healthy, incredible babies. The journey wasn't easy, but it was mine. It stretched me, refined me, and proved that the story I chose to tell myself shaped my reality.

Here's what I want you to take from my story: Every fear you carry has a lesson hidden within it. There's always a next level waiting for you, a place where your fear can be transformed into strength. Overcoming fear isn't about getting rid of it; it's about learning to coexist with it—about finding the power to keep moving forward even when you're scared.

So whether you're facing fears around your career, your relationships, or your personal dreams—know that there's a power inside you that fear can't touch. It will challenge you, yes, but it can also fuel your growth. And when you choose to confront your fears, you open the door to new possibilities, to abundance, and to the kind of growth you never imagined possible.

What I learned was that breaking these old habits wasn't easy, but it was necessary. I couldn't allow myself to stay stuck in the same cycles of fear that had held me back for so long. If I wanted to move forward—if I wanted to be the mother I needed to be for my children, the wife I needed to be for my husband, and the leader I needed to be in my business—I had to break free. I had to put those old habits to bed once and for all.

It wasn't about pretending the fear didn't exist, but about choosing to take action despite it. It was about embracing the unknown and trusting that I was capable of handling whatever came my way. And let me tell you: Once I made that shift, once I decided to break the cycle, everything started to change.

The fear didn't disappear, but it no longer had control over me. And that made all the difference.

So when you find yourself stuck in fear—whether it's the fear of rejection, the fear of failure, or the fear of not being enough—remember this: *Fear is not the enemy.* Fear is a teacher. It will show you where to dig deeper, where to heal, and where to expand. On the other side of fear is freedom.

And if I can push through my fears—if I can rewrite my narrative and change my story—I believe you can too.

_____
Unleash a new story of boldness, courage, and unstoppable optimism.
_____

Embracing Audacity: The Antidote to Fear

Here's an exercise I want you to do the next time you feel fear.

- **First, understand what you're actually afraid of.** Name it. Is it fear of failure? Fear that others will

reject you? Just giving it a name and pulling it into the light helps shrink its power.
- **Then identify the audacious action or goal that fear is trying to hold you back from.** What actions are you avoiding? What are you putting off? What is on the other side waiting for you if you had the audacious courage to overcome fear? Is it a career aspiration? Is it a personal dream? Visualize it.
- **Next, shift your focus from the potential risks to the potential rewards.** What could you gain by taking this step? What opportunities could open up?
- **Finally, move forward in spite of the fear.** Every time you take a step and overcome your fear, you strengthen your audacious muscle. And just like lifting weights, the next time is a little bit easier, and the time after that is easier still. You get stronger, more confident, and more audacious with practice.

A fear in motion will stay in motion—gathering momentum, feeding off doubt, and pushing you further into the shadows of your own limitations. But here's something equally true: Fear may obey the laws of inertia, but so does positive energy. And when you unleash a new story of boldness, courage, and unstoppable optimism, it collides with that fear and knocks it flat. Just like in physics, the force of your new narrative—driven by self-belief and purpose—overpowers the inertia of fear. It's not magic, it's momentum. Once you shift your focus

Audacious

and put that positive energy into motion, fear doesn't stand a chance. It's a cosmic law, and you're the one who rewrites it. Fear may be a natural part of the human experience, but it no longer has to define you. Face your fears and step into your audacious life story!

CHAPTER 2

The Magic of Vision

AUDACITY DARES YOU TO leap into the unknown, to chase what feels impossible—but vision gives you the map. It's the sacred ability to see beyond the limitations of today and paint a vivid picture of what could be. Without vision, boldness is aimless; with it, you unlock the extraordinary.

So what is vision? In the context of personal and professional development, vision is more than just a goal or a dream. It's a clear and compelling picture of the future you want to create. It's the ability to see possibilities where others see limitations. Vision is deeply personal; it reflects your values, your purpose, and your unique desires. It provides direction, acting as a compass that guides your decisions and fuels your persistence when the path gets tough.

Vision is the foundation for growth and success because it pushes you to think beyond the ordinary. It forces you to confront your fears, step out of your comfort zone, and take action even when the next step isn't obvious. A life lived without vision is reactive and stagnant, but a life fueled by vision is one of intentionality, progress, and fulfillment.

The genesis of my vision began in a moment of reflection and restlessness. I felt a deep yearning to create something meaningful—a life and career that not only fulfilled me but also impacted others. This vision didn't arrive fully formed. It started with small sparks: moments of inspiration, glimpses of what I wanted my life to look like, and the growing belief that I could create something greater than myself.

> Small beginnings are not a limitation; they're a foundation.

Audacious Truth #1: Dream Big, Even When You Have to Start Small

Here's the truth about vision: It doesn't require that everyone else sees what you see. It only requires that you believe it enough to begin. And beginning doesn't mean starting big—it means starting where you are, with what you have. Dreaming big often demands starting small. It's about taking that first tiny step while holding on to the larger picture in your heart. Small beginnings are not a limitation; they're a foundation. Each step forward builds momentum, and before you know it, what started as a small effort becomes something extraordinary.

When I launched my media company, Boss Women Media, I had a bold vision: to create a platform that empowered and connected women in meaningful ways. But like so many big dreams, it began with small, imperfect steps—and a lot of uncertainty. I didn't have a fully developed revenue plan. My initial strategy was simple: host events, sell tickets, and build from there. But it didn't take long to realize that relying on one unpredictable revenue stream wasn't sustainable.

About eight months in, I was staring down the reality of slow growth and financial strain. Revenue was trickling in, but it wasn't enough to cover expenses, let alone provide a stable income. Doubt started creeping in, and I questioned if I'd made the right decision to leave the security of a steady paycheck. I even considered picking up a retail job at Anthropologie just to make ends meet.

I was one click away from submitting an application when my husband stopped me. He reminded me why I had started this journey in the first place. "Building something meaningful takes time," he said. "Trust the process. Stay committed to your vision, and give it the space to grow. The money will come."

His words were the nudge I needed to refocus. I realized that dreaming big also means being patient—and creative—when the path gets rocky. I shifted my energy from worrying about quick fixes to exploring new opportunities. Instead of relying solely on events, I brainstormed fresh ways to generate revenue: collaborations, digital products, content sponsorships. Little by little, I began to diversify, and the vision I'd held onto started gaining momentum.

That season taught me one of the most valuable lessons of entrepreneurship: Dreaming big doesn't mean everything comes together at once. Dreaming big means daring to believe in the possibilities, even when the beginnings feel small. It's not about where you start but about the vision that keeps pulling you forward. Stay flexible and trust the process of slow, steady growth. Progress takes time, and the foundation you build in those early days—no matter how humble—paired with resilience and a willingness to adapt, is what ultimately turns small beginnings into big realities.

Audacious Truth #2: Dreaming with Others Is a Gift. It's Sharing Not Just a Vision of What Could Be, but a Journey of Becoming—Together.
After my first full year in business, buoyed by some significant successes, I entered year two with a renewed sense of confidence and momentum. This was 2019, and I was deep into planning my annual summit—a key event that I hoped would propel my brand even further. Although I hadn't yet secured major sponsorships, I was generating steady revenue with multiple $10,000 contracts from several brands. The summit was my chance to solidify that momentum, to grow the business into something bigger.

I was strategic about every detail, especially when it came to selecting the speakers. I wanted women who resonated not only with my brand but also with the larger vision I held. These were women who could see the potential of what I was building, who understood that with more investment, we could accomplish something powerful together. It was important to me that these speakers weren't just talking heads—they were women who believed in the mission of my company and saw its future impact.

To build that connection, I organized a private dinner with the speakers ahead of the summit. I wanted a chance to get to know them more intimately, to share my vision and show them what we could accomplish with their support. Over the course of the evening, as I shared my story, my goals, and the potential I saw for the brand, I could feel a shift happening. They weren't just listening—they were seeing it too. They understood the passion driving me and the impact this summit could have.

And then something incredible happened. After the dinner, several of these speakers approached me and, to my surprise, handed me personal checks—some for $7,500, others for $15,000. They didn't just want to support with their time and expertise; they wanted to invest in the vision financially. This wasn't just validation; it was a profound shift. It was one thing to have a vision and execute it, but to reach a point where people are willing to personally fund it—that's an entirely different level of success.

When people are inspired enough to invest in your dream, it's a signal that you've crossed a milestone. You've moved from an idea to something people believe in and want to see grow. This experience taught me a fundamental truth about entrepreneurship: Building something worthwhile isn't just about having a good idea; it's about bringing others into your vision so fully that they're willing to put their own resources behind it. That's a level of support every entrepreneur strives for—a testament to the power of shared belief, and a reminder that when others invest in your dream, it's no longer just yours alone. It's a shared mission with momentum beyond what you could have achieved on your own.

Entering that second year with a stronger network and financial backing from people who understood the journey made all the difference. It reaffirmed that a clear vision, combined with authenticity and strategy, can create a foundation others want to help build upon.

Casting a vision is about creating a clear, compelling, and inspiring mental image of what's possible—not just for you,

> It's about bringing others into your vision so fully that they're willing to put their own resources behind it.

but for the people and communities your vision will impact. A well-cast vision doesn't just live in your mind; it inspires others to see it, believe in it, and join you in making it real.

Audacious Truth #3: Be Alert and Open to Adjacent Opportunities While You Build Your Vision

Sometimes, the most transformative opportunities come from the places you least expect. During one of the most challenging periods of my journey, I learned this firsthand. While my media company was in its infancy and had a few people starting to invest, I was still figuring out how to sustain it. Revenue was slow, and doubt crept in daily. Amid this uncertainty, I had a coffee meeting scheduled with the First Lady of my church. My intention for the meeting was simple: share the vision for my company, honor her at an upcoming event, and begin building a meaningful connection.

I hoped she'd accept the invitation to the event. What I didn't expect was that this one conversation would change the course of my life.

As I sat across from her, passionately explaining my dream for the company and my vision for creating spaces of empowerment and connection, she listened intently. When I finished, she smiled warmly and said something that completely caught me off guard: "We could really use someone like you on our team."

Her words were a balm for my weary spirit. After years of corporate experiences where my creativity and talents were often overlooked, hearing her validate my skills and value felt like a breakthrough. I hadn't realized how much I needed to hear that, how much I needed to be reminded of my worth.

That conversation opened the door to an adjacent opportunity I hadn't been looking for. Soon after, I met with the church's HR team, sharing my skills and passion for communication and connection. To my surprise, they embraced my unique perspective and invited me to join their women's ministry team as a contractor.

This role became a turning point. It wasn't just a chance to contribute—it was a chance to grow. For the first time, I found myself in an environment that celebrated my creativity, welcomed my ideas, and encouraged me to lean into my strengths. The projects I took on, the meetings I led, and the impacts I made were not only fulfilling, they reminded me of who I was and what I was capable of.

While I continued building my business, this opportunity served as a lifeline. It allowed me to sustain myself financially, but more than that, it became a space to refine and strengthen my gifts simultaneously. It was like a training ground for the vision I was building, giving me the confidence to believe more fully in myself and my dream.

Looking back, I see now that this wasn't just a job—it was a moment of divine alignment. It reminded me that staying open to adjacent opportunities doesn't mean abandoning your vision; it means embracing the paths that strengthen and support it. Sometimes, those opportunities provide the resources, the skills, or the confidence you need to bring your big dreams to life.

That coffee meeting taught me a vital truth: While dreaming big, you must remain alert to the opportunities around you. They may not look exactly like what you imagined, but they might be exactly what you need to fuel your journey forward. Be audacious enough to see the possibilities—and bold enough to say yes.

Audacious Truth #4: Go After Bold, Audacious Goals (B.A.G.)
In 2019, I found myself sitting in my friend's living room, talking about my goals for 2020. My dreams were bold—so bold they made my heart race. I spoke passionately about the impact I wanted to create, the connections I envisioned, and the transformative programming I planned to launch. Then, I shared an idea that had taken root in my heart: I wanted to host a brunch to celebrate one hundred dynamic women from across the United States on International Women's Day.

The event would honor their achievements and provide a space for them to connect and inspire one another. I envisioned flying them in that morning, hosting them for an unforgettable gathering, and sending them back home by evening. I even had the name ready: **100 Women Sitting at the Table.** As I described the vision, I could feel its energy. I could see the women's faces and sense the connections they'd build.

But when I glanced at the people around me—my friends and even my husband—their expressions told a different story. Skepticism hung in the air. They politely asked practical questions: *How will you get one hundred women there? Who would they be? Why would they come?* Their doubt was palpable.

Even so, I held firm. The vision was clear to me, and no amount of doubt could shake it. I understood something then

The Magic of Vision

that has stayed with me: Not everyone will see your vision, and that's okay.

In spite of the doubt around me—and moments of my own self-doubt—I got to work. Time was short, and it was already November 2019, with March 2020 fast approaching. I mapped out logistics, made countless phone calls, and shared my vision with anyone who would listen. Every day, I chipped away at the mountain of tasks, fueled by an unshakable belief that this event wasn't just for me—it was for the women who needed a seat at that table.

By March 7, 2020—just before the world shut down due to the COVID-19 pandemic—I had achieved what others doubted. **100 Women Sitting at the Table** became a reality. Women from across the country gathered, connected, and celebrated one another's achievements. The energy in the room was electric, and the impact was undeniable. Even the friends who doubted me in the beginning were there, helping to transport women from the airport to the venue.

That moment wasn't just about proving the doubters wrong. It was about the power of pursuing bold audacious goals.

What Makes a Goal Audacious?

The idea of flying in one hundred women was what I like to call a **Bold Audacious Goal (B.A.G.)**—a dream so bold it stretches your imagination and pushes you beyond what feels comfortable.

Here's what defines an audacious goal:

1. **It feels impossible (at first).** An audacious goal isn't something you already know how to achieve. It's the

kind of goal that makes your heart race and your mind question, *Can I really do this?*
2. **It aligns with your values and purpose.** Audacious goals are deeply personal. They reflect what matters most to you and what you're called to contribute to the world.
3. **It challenges you to grow.** The pursuit of an audacious goal will require new skills, new thinking, and new levels of perseverance. It's less about the destination and more about who you become along the way.
4. **It inspires and energizes you.** When you think about this goal, it ignites a spark within you. It excites you, even if it also terrifies you a little.
5. **It impacts more than just you.** Truly audacious goals often ripple outward, touching the lives of others and creating a positive impact in your community or the world.
6. **It requires faith and commitment.** An audacious goal isn't achieved overnight. It demands that you stay committed, even when the path is unclear, and trust that the process will unfold in the right way.

Audacious goals stretch you beyond your comfort zone, challenge your limits, and push the boundaries of what you believe is possible. They require courage, resilience, and a vision deeply aligned with your purpose. More than just being big or impressive, audacious goals are beacons—guiding you toward transformative growth and calling you to rise as your best self.

The Magic of Vision

Exercise: Write Down Your B.A.G.

What would you attempt if you truly believed there were no limits? This question isn't rhetorical—it's an invitation to dream boldly. Here's an exercise to help you identify your Bold Audacious Goals.

1. Take a moment to reflect on your life—your dreams, your purpose, and the impact you want to make. Then, write down one Bold Audacious Goal that feels impossible right now but excites you deeply.
2. Underneath your goal, answer these questions:
    - Why does this goal matter to me?
    - What fears or doubts come up when I think about pursuing it?
    - Who could be positively impacted if I achieve this goal?
3. Break it down into one small, actionable step you can take today. Remember, even the boldest goals start with a single step.

Audacious goals are not just for the fearless; they're for the determined. They're for those who dare to dream bigger than their circumstances, who believe in their vision even when others can't see it yet. Your B.A.G. is waiting—will you go after it?

Audacious Truth #5: Don't Be Afraid to Pivot to Accomplish Your Dreams
In 2020, the same year as the 100 Women event, I was on the verge of something monumental. I had spent years nurturing

a vision that felt larger than life—a vision to create spaces for women to come together, be inspired, and unlock their potential. That vision was finally about to become a reality with a seven-city tour called Black Girl Magic. The dream was backed by a six-figure sponsorship deal with a major financial institution—a milestone I had worked tirelessly to achieve. It was more than an event; it was a movement to empower and uplift women across the country. It was everything I had imagined, and I was ready to make an impact on women's lives.

But then, the world changed.

The pandemic swept in and disrupted everything. What was initially planned as a series of live events to connect women in vibrant, energizing spaces suddenly became impossible. The cancellations came in, one after another. Months of preparation, late nights, and pitching seemed to dissolve overnight.

At first, I felt like I was simply hitting a speed bump, but as the days turned into weeks, it became clear that I wasn't just navigating a minor setback—I was facing a mountain. The tour couldn't move forward as planned, and it felt like the vision I had poured so much into was slipping away.

> **To dream audaciously is to believe in the "what" even when the "how" feels uncertain.**

Still, quitting wasn't an option. I had worked too hard, and the impact I wanted to create was too important. I had to find another way.

The Pivot: Reimagining the Vision

I went into problem-solving mode, scouring the internet and researching how other brands were transitioning to virtual events. But I knew that a traditional online event—a basic Zoom

The Magic of Vision

call—wouldn't capture the essence of what Black Girl Magic was meant to be. This wasn't just about hosting an event; it was about delivering an experience that felt just as powerful and transformative online as it would have in person.

I worked with my team to brainstorm ideas and reached out to the sponsor to propose a new plan: a virtual summit reimagined for a digital audience. It would coincide with Black Business Month in August—a perfect fit for the event's mission to celebrate and elevate Black women.

The pivot wasn't without challenges. I had committed to bringing in five thousand women for this virtual summit. But as the date approached, fear set in. What if no one showed up? What if all of this effort was for nothing?

Those doubts were quickly silenced as the registrations rolled in. By the end of the first week, over 7,500 women had signed up. By the time registration closed, the number had soared to more than **twenty-two thousand women from thirty-three different countries.**

The event itself was electric. Women tuned in from across the globe to hear stories, gain insights, and connect with one another in ways they never thought possible. The virtual platform became a space of inspiration and empowerment, proving that even in the face of the unexpected, the magic could still happen.

What started as a seven-city tour became a global movement. The vision was always big, but the pivot allowed it to reach farther and touch more lives than I ever imagined. The success of Black Girl Magic wasn't just about numbers; it was about the lives it touched and the communities it brought together. Women shared stories of how the event gave them clarity, courage, and tools to take bold steps in their own lives.

This experience taught me the power of holding on to a bold vision while remaining flexible in its execution. Dreaming big doesn't mean everything will go as planned—it means staying committed to the impact you want to create, even when the route changes.

To dream audaciously is to believe in the "what" even when the "how" feels uncertain. It's about being willing to pivot, to reimagine, and to push forward in the face of obstacles. This is the essence of dreaming big. Now let's talk about how you can activate your audacious vision with some practical how-to strategies.

Activating Your Audacious Vision

Activating a vision is about creating a clear, compelling, and inspiring mental image of what's possible—not just for you, but for the people and communities your vision will impact. A well-cast vision doesn't just live in your mind; it inspires others to see it, believe in it, and join you in making it real. Here are some practical ways you can activate your audacious vision.

Step 1: Create a Clear Vision
Your vision should be so vivid and compelling that it fills you with excitement and passion. Use one or more of these methods to start crafting it:

- **Write It Down/Journaling:** Spend time reflecting on your goals. Write a detailed description of what success looks like, feels like, and even sounds like. Be specific—clarity is key.

- **Visualization:** Close your eyes and imagine your future in detail. Picture the people, places, and experiences that are part of your vision. Let yourself feel the emotions tied to it—joy, pride, excitement.
- **Vision Boards:** Gather images, quotes, and symbols that represent your vision and create a visual representation. Keep it somewhere where you can see it daily.
- **Collaboration and Mentorship:** Talk to trusted mentors, colleagues, or friends. Share your vision and invite their insights. But remember—while input is valuable, stay grounded in your core vision. Don't let outside voices dilute your clarity.

Step 2: Share Your Vision

Your vision isn't just for you—it's a rallying cry for others to join you. Once you've crafted your vision, practice sharing it in a way that is passionate, clear, and inspiring.

Ask yourself:

- *Does my vision reflect a future bigger than myself?*
- *Can others see themselves in the picture I'm painting?*
- *Am I conveying not just the "what," but also the "why" behind my vision?*

Step 3: Invite Others to Believe in It

A strong vision compels others to take action, whether that's offering support, collaborating with you, or even investing in your dream. Challenge yourself to identify people who could be inspired by your vision and invite them into the journey.

Step 4: Take Inspired Action
A vision without action is just a dream. Break your vision into actionable steps, starting small if necessary. Each step you take toward your vision builds momentum and brings it closer to reality.

How to Handle Doubt—Yours and Theirs

One thing I get asked a lot is: "What do you do when your dream seems 'too audacious'? How do you overcome self-doubt and other people's disbelief?" Here's the reality: Even when you take all of these steps to activate your vision and be clear about it, not everyone will believe in your vision. That's okay. Some people will doubt because they can't see what you see, and others may project their own fears onto your dream. Some may not even want to see you succeed.

And as challenging as dealing with the doubt of others is, sometimes what's harder is dealing with our own doubt. Even I have had moments of self-doubt throughout my journey. There were nights when I wondered, *Can I really pull this off? What if no one shows up?* But I kept coming back to the vision. I reminded myself why I started and focused on the impact I wanted to create. You must do the same for your vision. Doubt is not a sign to quit. It's a sign to strengthen your belief in yourself.

Here are some practical steps I use to strengthen my self-belief and overcome doubt—both my own and that of others.

The Magic of Vision

1. **Ground Yourself in the Vision.** Write it down. Make it so clear and compelling that it fills you with excitement every time you read it.
2. **Start Small.** Break your big goal into actionable steps. Focus on progress, not perfection.
3. **Find Your Champions.** Surround yourself with people who believe in you and your vision. Their encouragement can help drown out the doubters.
4. **Accept That Not Everyone Will Understand.** Your vision doesn't need universal approval to succeed.
5. **Use Doubt as Fuel.** Let skepticism motivate you to prove what's possible.

> Doubt is not a sign to quit. It's a sign to strengthen your belief in yourself.

Pursue Your Vision Audaciously

Dreaming big isn't just about setting goals—it's about who you become in the process. When you dare to pursue a Bold Audacious Goal, you open the door to transformation, not just for yourself but for everyone your dream touches.

So write down your B.A.G. Share it with someone. Get to work activating it. Remember, the world needs your vision, even if others can't see it yet. The only question is: Will you dare to pursue it audaciously?

Audacity fuels the action that makes the vision real. The two are inseparable; together, they are the foundation of a fulfilling life and career. The life you want, the change you hope to see, the legacy you dream of leaving—all of it begins with a vision. But to bring that vision to life, you must be

Audacious

audacious enough to take the first step, even when the road ahead is uncertain. Your vision matters. It has the power to shape your life and the lives of those around you. Embrace it, nurture it, and let your audacity drive you to make it real.

The world is waiting for what only you can create. Now is the time to begin. Step into your audacious vision.

CHAPTER 3

Flip the Script and Rewrite Your Story

IN 2021, AFTER THE birth of my first daughter, my life felt like a heavy fog that I couldn't escape. Everything seemed out of focus, and I felt like I was wading through mental quicksand. I couldn't think clearly, my decision-making was completely off, and I felt paralyzed by a deep sense of overwhelm. It wasn't just the demands of motherhood; it was as though I had lost my sense of self. I knew I should be doing more, but I couldn't figure out how—or even where—to start.

If you've ever felt like this, you know how disorienting it can be. You start to second-guess everything, and even the smallest tasks feel monumental. For me, this spiral was fueled by the unrealistic expectations I placed on myself—to be a perfect mother, to keep up at work, and to juggle everything seamlessly. But beneath those expectations was a deeper issue: the stories I had been telling myself.

I had convinced myself that I had to do it all alone, that asking for help was a sign of weakness, and that admitting I was struggling meant I was failing. These beliefs weren't just holding me back—they were suffocating me. I hadn't shared how I was feeling with anyone outside of my husband, but he could tell something was off. He could see it in my eyes, in the way I was trying to hold everything together but clearly failing. One day, he suggested something unexpected. He showed me a clip from a performance coach on Instagram. "What do you think about reaching out to her?" he asked.

My initial reaction was immediate rejection. "She works with real estate agents," I scoffed. "What could she possibly teach me?" My mind was closed, trapped by the narrative that seeking help wasn't for someone like me. But then I caught myself. What was I really afraid of? The truth was, I wasn't just afraid of hiring a coach. I was afraid of confronting the stories that were keeping me stuck—the fear that perhaps I wasn't good enough? Or maybe that asking for help meant I had failed in some way? If you know anything about me, you know I'm an **Enneagram Type Eight**. Eights are called The Challengers, and we're known for being self-confident, assertive, and strong-willed. At our core, we value control—specifically, control over our lives and our environments. For someone like me, the idea of letting someone else in to help felt like a loss of control, and honestly, a big part of me resisted the very idea. But deep down, I knew that I couldn't do it all alone anymore. If I continued trying to "fix" everything on my own, I would only end up overwhelmed, burned out, and increasingly frustrated.

When I finally reached out to the coach, it wasn't an easy process. Her program was a significant investment, and I almost backed out entirely. But as I sat with my hesitation, I realized something profound: My resistance wasn't about the money. It was about fear. I was afraid of failing. I was afraid of proving my story right—that I wasn't capable, that I wasn't worthy of success. But what if I was wrong?

I decided to take the leap. In our first session, my coach asked a question that stopped me in my tracks: "What's the narrative you're living by right now?" I had never thought of my inner dialogue as a narrative before. But as I unpacked my thoughts, I saw how much power those stories had over my life.

The breakthrough came when I opened up about my frustrations in securing partnerships and sponsorships. I told her how I felt unseen and undervalued because of my audience—primarily Black women. "Companies don't prioritize us," I said. "They don't see our worth." I expected her to comfort me, but instead, she challenged me. "What if you rewrote that story?" she asked. "What if you focused on the organizations that align with your values, that believe in what you're building?"

It was like a light bulb went off. For so long, I had been fixated on the wrong things—on the companies that didn't value me—when I had the power to seek out and attract the ones that did. By shifting my narrative, I opened the door to new possibilities. And once I embraced this new story, everything changed.

Within a year, I went from having a consistent six-figure income to breaking into seven figures. The difference wasn't that I worked harder or suddenly figured out a magical formula. The difference was the story I told myself. I stopped operating from a place of fear and scarcity, and I started acting from a mindset of possibility and abundance.

The lesson here is powerful: The stories we tell ourselves shape our reality.

Identifying Your Story

That's the thing about stories—they're so deeply ingrained in us that we often don't even realize they're there. Think about it. How often have you heard—or told yourself—a narrative like this:

- *I'm not good enough.*
- *I'm not worthy of success.*
- *I'm not capable of achieving my dreams.*
- *I don't deserve happiness.*

These aren't just fleeting thoughts. They're stories we repeat to ourselves, often without even realizing it. Over time, they become the lens through which we view everything. They shape our decisions, our relationships, and the opportunities we pursue—or avoid.

For me, one of my most persistent narratives was *I have to do it all on my own*. This belief stemmed from a lifetime of striving for independence and pride in being self-reliant. But what I didn't see was how this story was limiting me. It kept me from asking for help when I needed it most. It left me feeling isolated, overwhelmed, and stuck.

The Roots of Our Narratives

Our narratives don't just appear out of nowhere. They're formed by the layers of our lives:

- **Experiences:** A past failure might lead you to believe you're not capable. A difficult relationship might convince you that you're unlovable.
- **Beliefs:** Whether inherited from family or developed through personal experiences, beliefs shape our core understanding of what's possible.
- **Words from others:** A critical comment from a teacher, a dismissive remark from a peer, or even well-meaning advice can plant seeds of doubt.
- **Societal influences:** Cultural norms and media can reinforce ideas about what we should or shouldn't aspire to.
- **Life's challenges:** When life doesn't go as planned, it's easy to internalize those struggles as personal shortcomings.

These influences combine to create the stories we tell ourselves, and they shape the way we see ourselves and the world around us. And once those narratives take root, they become self-fulfilling prophecies.

Identifying Your Narrative

Now that you understand where our stories come from, it's time to examine the one you're living by. **What story are you**

telling yourself right now? Take a moment to reflect. If it's a story that's keeping you stuck, ask yourself: *How can I rewrite this narrative?* You have the power to reshape your reality by reshaping your story. Take a moment to explore these prompts and write down your thoughts:

1. **What story are you currently telling yourself?**
   Reflect on the narrative running in the background of your life. Is it a story of possibility or one of limitation?
2. **What are the recurring themes in your thoughts and self-talk?**
   Do you find yourself thinking, *I'm not good enough*, or *I always mess things up*? Pay attention to the patterns that keep showing up.
3. **What beliefs do you hold about your abilities, worth, and potential?**
   Be honest with yourself. Do you believe you're capable of achieving your goals? Or do you secretly doubt your worthiness of success?
4. **What stories do you tell yourself about your past experiences?**
   Look at how you interpret your failures and setbacks. Do you see them as evidence that you'll never succeed? Or as lessons that can propel you forward?
5. **Is your story keeping you from an audacious life?**
   Think about the dreams you've put on hold or the risks you've avoided. How has your narrative influenced those choices?

Is Your Story Keeping You from an Audacious Life?

Our limiting narratives act like invisible barriers. They keep us from pursuing bold goals, taking risks, or stepping outside of our comfort zones—the very actions needed to live an audacious life. For example:

- If you believe, *I'm not capable of achieving my dreams,* you might avoid applying for a new role or starting a business you've always dreamed of.
- If you tell yourself, *I don't deserve happiness,* you might settle for relationships, jobs, or situations that don't truly fulfill you.
- If you're stuck in the narrative of *I'm not good enough,* you might hesitate to showcase your talents, even when opportunities arise.

These stories aren't just harmless thoughts—they shape the reality you live in. If your narrative is one of fear, inadequacy, or scarcity, you'll make choices that reinforce those beliefs. If you tell yourself you're not good enough, you'll live a life that reflects that belief. But if you change your story—if you choose to see yourself as capable, worthy, and deserving—you'll create a life that reflects those truths. The good news is, you have the power to rewrite your story and break free from these limitations.

Strategies to Rewrite Your Narrative

Rewriting your narrative doesn't happen overnight, but with intentional effort, you can reshape the story that guides your life. Here are eight actionable strategies to help you start:

1. **Identify and Challenge Your Limiting Beliefs.**
   Write down the negative stories you tell yourself. Then, ask: *Is this belief absolutely true?* Look for evidence to disprove it. For example, if you believe, *I'm not good enough,* write down all the ways you've proven your abilities in the past.
2. **Reframe Your Self-Talk.**
   Start noticing the way you speak to yourself. Replace negative phrases like *I can't do this* with empowering ones like *I'm learning how to do this.* Over time, these small shifts will change the way you see yourself.
3. **Focus on What You Can Control.**
   Many of our limiting narratives stem from focusing on external factors we can't change. Instead, shift your attention to what's within your power. For example, instead of saying, *No one values my work,* focus on *I will connect with people who align with my values.*
4. **Revisit Your Past Through a New Lens.**
   Look back at moments of failure or hardship. Instead of seeing them as evidence of inadequacy, reinterpret them as experiences that taught you resilience and wisdom. Ask yourself: *What did I learn? How did this make me stronger?*

5. **Create a New Affirmative Narrative.**
   Write down a new story about yourself—one rooted in possibility. For example:
   - Old story: *I'm not capable of success.*
   - New story: *I have the skills, passion, and determination to succeed.*
6. **Surround Yourself with Positive Influences.**
   The people and environments you engage with can either reinforce or challenge your limiting beliefs. Seek out communities, mentors, or friends who inspire and support your growth.
7. **Take Small, Audacious Steps.**
   Every time you take action that contradicts your limiting narrative, you weaken its hold. Start with small, bold actions—apply for that opportunity, share your ideas, or reach out to someone you admire. Over time, these steps will build confidence in your new story.
8. **Celebrate Your Wins—Big and Small.**
   Acknowledge your progress, no matter how small it feels. Celebrating your successes reinforces the belief that you're capable and worthy of achieving your goals.

Your New Story Begins Now

Flipping the script on your narrative isn't just about changing your mindset—it's about reshaping your entire reality. By taking ownership of your story, you're choosing to live with intention, clarity, and purpose. You're choosing to break free from the chains of fear and step into an audacious life.

So I'll ask you again: *What story are you currently telling yourself?* And more importantly, how will you rewrite it? Take the time to reflect, write it down, and start leaning into the narrative that reflects the person you're becoming.

CHAPTER 4

The Comparison Trap

I HAVE BEEN COMPARING myself to others for as long as I can remember. It started in elementary school, back when I thought the girl sitting two rows over had the perfect backpack, the perfect handwriting, and, somehow, the perfect life. I didn't know her struggles or her story—what I saw was enough to convince me that she had something I didn't.

That feeling followed me like a shadow through my childhood and beyond, always whispering that I needed *more*. More approval. More recognition. More of what someone else had. The comparisons grew louder as I grew older. From friendships to achievements to the paths others were walking, I constantly measured myself against others and wondered why I didn't stack up.

This constant comparison made me spend so much time looking outward, wishing I had someone else's life. I'd observe other families, imagining their parents with Ivy League degrees, an endless stream of resources, a beautiful home, vacations to places like Martha's Vineyard, and their seemingly effortless connections, and feel a pang of inadequacy. I dreamed of a life free from worry about my next meal or where I was going to sleep at night, a life of privilege and ease. I longed for a reality that felt far removed from my own. I was so focused on what I *lacked*—the stability, the resources, the picture-perfect image—that I was completely blind to what I *had*. I was so busy looking at everyone else's lives, I was missing my own.

Looking back in retrospect today, I am so grateful I didn't grow up in that world. I didn't grow up with the kind of privilege people often imagine when they see someone "making it"—and I certainly didn't grow up with a straight path toward success.

No, I grew up in Murfreesboro, Tennessee, in the '90s, one of the first biracial kids in my community. My family life was unstable and we moved frequently, making it hard to feel grounded. From kindergarten to fourth grade, I attended three different schools, constantly feeling like an outsider.

It wasn't until much later that I realized something profound: While I was busy comparing myself to others, someone else was looking at *me* and seeing something special. They saw strengths, potential, and a unique spark that I was too preoccupied to notice. I was so invested in my own perceived lack that I missed the fact that someone else saw my abundance.

One of those people was my second-grade teacher, Mr. Campbell. He was loud, funny, full of life, and he had this wild collection of button-down shirts that always seemed a little out of place. He wasn't just a teacher; he was an advocate. He had this unique way of making me feel seen, of affirming my worth even when I couldn't see it myself. Every time he called on me, he would sing out my name with a big smile and shout, "The most beautiful girl in the world!" At the time it was embarrassing, but now I understand: While I was wishing for a different life, he was showing me the beauty in the one I already had.

But here's what I've learned: Comparison dims your light. It blinds you to your own blessings and keeps you from feeling grateful for what you already have. It takes your focus off the things that make your life beautiful and unique, instead convincing you that you're falling short. For years, I let comparison steal my joy. I let it make me feel small. It's easy to look at someone else's life and think, *Why don't I have that? Why does she have it so easy? Why hasn't it happened for me yet?* It's easy to compare. But let me tell you: Comparison is the thief of all joy.

Now, I see it for what it is—a trap—and I have learned how to overcome it and walk in my uniqueness and calling. What if you could break free too, allowing your light to shine unfiltered and undimmed? *Let's discover how.* It's time to stop comparing and start embracing the power of gratitude, self-acceptance, and the audacity to live your own story. *Let's step into that truth.*

The Impact of Comparison: How It Stifles Audacity

Have you ever caught yourself scrolling through social media, seeing someone's carefully curated highlight reel, and suddenly feeling as though your own life is inadequate? Maybe it's the friend who just got engaged, the couple celebrating their anniversary in Bali, or the coworker who seems to be crushing it in their career while you're struggling to get through the day. That quiet, creeping feeling of comparison begins to take root, and before you know it, you're questioning your own journey, your goals, and even your worth.

You might be wondering why I'm dedicating an entire chapter to comparison in a book about audacity. But here's the truth: Comparison is one of the most insidious forces that stifles audacity. It keeps you small, stops you from taking risks, and prevents you from pursuing your unique path. Comparison and audacity cannot coexist, because to be audacious requires believing in your ability to create your own path—something that becomes nearly impossible when you're fixated on someone else's.

> Fulfillment doesn't come from copying someone else's journey; it comes from walking your own path.

Don't Compare—Just Smile and Enjoy Your Ride

When I was starting my business I would sit for hours, staring at the ceiling, wondering when it would finally be my time. When would the deals come? When would I find the right partners? When would the opportunities, recognition, and success start flowing my way? I had big dreams—huge dreams—but the waiting game was brutal. And what made it even harder was the constant comparison.

I'd watch other women—entrepreneurs, influencers, people I admired—seemingly living the life I wanted. Social media didn't help. Research indicates a significant correlation between social media usage and negative mental health outcomes among adults. I'd scroll through highlight reels of perfect launches, stunning brands, and flawless lives. Meanwhile, I felt like I was barely keeping it together. Each post I saw whispered the same lie: *You're not enough. You're behind.* That, my friend, is the thief of joy. Comparison clouds your vision, steals your happiness, and leaves you feeling small.

The Comparison Trap

Here is what will happen if you focus on comparison:

1. **Losing Focus on Your Goals**

When you're caught up in comparison, your focus shifts away from your own personal goals and values. Instead, you start chasing someone else's dreams, thinking that if you achieve what they have, you'll feel the same sense of fulfillment. But here's the hard truth: You won't. Fulfillment doesn't come from copying someone else's journey; it comes from walking your own path.

2. **Believing in the Illusion of "One Big Goal"**

Comparison often feeds the illusion that there's one ultimate goal to reach, one magical destination where all your dreams will come true. This is a lie. I used to think that once I had reached that next level—once I had hit that one major milestone, once I had achieved that one goal—I would finally be satisfied. But here's the truth: Once you hit one goal, there's always another waiting. Life isn't about arriving at some mythical endpoint where you've finally "made it." If you keep thinking that happiness is tied to the next thing, you will forever be chasing something that can never truly satisfy you. Happiness doesn't come from achieving goals; it comes from finding contentment in the process. It's about the journey, the growth, and the joy you find along the way.

3. **Creating Limiting Beliefs**

Comparison breeds limiting beliefs. When you see someone else achieving something, it's easy to fall into the trap of thinking,

Audacious

That's not possible for me. You start to believe that success, joy, or love are finite—that if someone else has them, there's less available for you. But this scarcity mindset is the enemy of audacity. Being audacious requires believing that abundance is available to everyone, including you.

4. Robbing You of Joy

Ultimately, comparison robs you of joy. It blinds you to the blessings in your own life and fills you with feelings of inadequacy and envy. But here's the thing: You can't be audacious and envious at the same time. Audacity comes from a place of confidence, gratitude, and abundance, not scarcity and lack.

> You can't be audacious and envious at the same time.

Here's the good news: You don't have to live in a state of continual comparison. Over time, I learned to let go of comparison, embrace gratitude, and step fully into my own journey, and you can too!

Ways to Overcome Comparison—Cultivating Self-Acceptance and Audacity

I want to share with you the eight strategies that helped me overcome comparison and cultivate self-acceptance. These are the keys that unlock an audacious life:

Strategy #1: Celebrate Your Strengths and Uniqueness
When you're stuck in the comparison trap, it's easy to focus on what you *don't* have. But I want you to pause and think about

what makes you uniquely *you*. Your story, your experiences, your perspective—those are your superpowers. No one else can bring to the table what you bring.

For me, starting Boss Women Media was about filling a gap I noticed in the marketplace. I realized my experiences and vision were valuable because they were uniquely mine. Instead of comparing myself to others, I leaned into my strengths and trusted that my voice mattered. And yours does too.

Strategy #2: Express Gratitude
Comparison makes you focus on what's missing, but gratitude shifts your attention to what you already have. It's a powerful tool for grounding yourself in the present and cultivating joy.

Here's a quick exercise: Write down five things you're grateful for right now. It could be something big, like the people who believe in your dreams, or something small, like a warm cup of coffee. Gratitude trains your mind to see abundance rather than scarcity. And when you're rooted in abundance, comparison loses its grip.

Strategy #3: Use Their Success as Motivation
I used to feel crushed when I saw someone else achieving something I wanted. But then I had a revelation: If they can do it, so can I. Their success isn't a threat—it's proof that what I want is possible.

When you see someone living the life you aspire to, let it fuel your fire. Instead of thinking, *Why not me?* shift your mindset to, *It's possible for me too.* Celebrate their wins as a reminder that there's enough room at the table for everyone—including you.

Audacious

Strategy #4: Believe That Your Timing Is Perfect
One of the hardest lessons I've learned is this: Your timing is your own. Trust it. What's meant for you will not pass you by. I used to think I was running out of time, especially when I saw others achieving milestones I hadn't reached yet. But the truth is that life isn't a race.

When I started trusting that my journey was unfolding exactly as it should, I found peace. Your time is coming. Stay consistent, stay committed, and trust the process.

> Chasing "more" keeps you stuck in a cycle of dissatisfaction. Instead, focus on the now.

Strategy #5: Shift from More to Now
We live in a world that glorifies "more"—more success, more followers, more money. But chasing "more" keeps you stuck in a cycle of dissatisfaction. Instead, focus on the now.

Celebrate where you are today. Acknowledge the progress you've made, no matter how small. If you're always comparing yourself to someone else, or tirelessly striving for more, you'll miss the beauty of contentment right where you are. Here's a powerful truth: Contentment and comparison cannot coexist. You can either experience one or the other. Contentment doesn't mean complacency. It doesn't mean you stop pursuing your dreams. It simply means you find joy in the journey, even when you're not at the finish line yet.

Strategy #6: Be Intentional
Comparison often happens when we're not intentional with our focus. We get distracted by what others are doing and lose

sight of our own goals. To overcome this, you must be deliberate about how you spend your time and energy.

Every morning, I ask myself: *What can I do today to move closer to my dreams?* That simple question keeps me grounded and focused. When you're intentional about your actions, you stop worrying about others and start prioritizing what truly matters to you.

Strategy #7: Stop Waiting for Permission
One of the most freeing lessons I've learned is this: **You don't need anyone's permission to live boldly.** You don't need to wait for the perfect moment or for someone to validate your dreams. The only person who can give you permission to go after what you want is *you*.

> You don't need anyone's permission to live boldly.

So stop hesitating. Stop doubting. Show up for yourself, right now. Your journey is yours to claim—don't let fear or comparison hold you back.

Strategy #8: Enjoy the Ride
At the end of the day, the journey is the reward. Every challenge, every win, every lesson—it's all part of the beautiful ride. Comparison will try to distract you, but don't let it. Stay focused on your path, and find joy in every step along the way.

Letting go of comparison isn't easy, but it's worth it. When you stop measuring yourself against others, you create space for gratitude, growth, and audacity. Your journey is your own, and it's unfolding exactly as it should. Remember these eight strategies. Lean into them. And most importantly, enjoy your ride.

Audacious

The Audacity to Be You—Living Beyond Comparison

Overcoming comparison isn't just about freeing yourself from negativity; it's about stepping fully into the audacity to be you. Audacity isn't loud or boastful—it's quiet, grounded, and deeply rooted in self-acceptance and self-belief. It's about recognizing that you are enough, just as you are, and that your path is uniquely yours to walk.

True audacity begins within. It grows when you stop chasing someone else's version of success and start embracing your own individuality. When you stop comparing, you give yourself permission to dream boldly, pursue your passions unapologetically, and find joy in the journey.

Here's the truth: No one else has your story, your vision, or your gifts. The world needs what you bring to the table—not a copy of someone else, but the full, authentic, audacious *you*. Celebrate your uniqueness, and let that celebration fuel your journey forward.

Now is the time to take the next step toward living an audacious life. Stop waiting for the perfect moment. Stop looking sideways. Look inward, find your strength, and let it guide you. Let go of comparison, embrace your individuality, and pursue your dreams with gratitude and contentment.

The ride ahead won't always be easy, but it will always be yours. And that's what makes it extraordinary. So go forward with audacity. Trust in your timing, lean into your strengths, and live boldly. The best is yet to come.

You've got this—now go and be unapologetically *you*.

CHAPTER 5

Shifting from Scarcity to Abundance

THERE'S A POINT IN your life when you realize that everything you've been doing has been based on a lie—a mindset that's been holding you back. For many of us, that moment comes in the form of a job, a relationship, or a big decision. And for me, that turning point happened in 2016, when I found myself working for a notable brand, in what many would consider a "dream job." But it wasn't until I left that role, broken but enlightened, that I truly understood the power of a **scarcity mindset versus an abundance mindset.**

This isn't just a corporate story; this is about life, identity, and the moments that define who we are. It's about how the mindset you choose can shape your success, happiness, and even your future. If there's anything I want you to take away from my story, it's this: Believing in abundance is the game-changer

> **Believing in abundance is the game-changer that will unlock the most audacious life you've ever known.**

that will unlock the most audacious life you've ever known.

The Illusion of the "Dream Job"

In 2016, I was at the peak of what I thought was my career. I had just accepted a position as the marketing manager for a notable brand. This was the job I had spent years working toward—a job where I would oversee both national and local marketing campaigns, work closely with high-end brands, and, most importantly, travel the world. For someone who had always dreamed of being in a powerful marketing role, this felt like the culmination of all my efforts. I was finally here.

But what no one tells you is that even when you think you've "made it," the journey has just begun. I was excited and nervous in equal measure, but there was an underlying feeling I couldn't shake off. I was determined to do my best, to prove my worth, but deep down I wasn't sure if I truly belonged. **I had worked so hard to get here, but the truth was, I didn't feel fully prepared to own it.**

From day one, I felt the weight of expectation on my shoulders. I was a young Black woman stepping into a leadership role in an industry that wasn't known for being diverse, let alone welcoming. In fact, when I looked around, I saw that I was the only Black woman working at the company. I didn't notice it right away, but it didn't take long for that absence to weigh heavily on me.

The lack of diversity, although subtle at first, soon became one of the most glaring aspects of my experience. There was

Shifting from Scarcity to Abundance

no one who looked like me, who understood my experience, or who could speak to the challenges I was silently facing. I felt isolated, and in many ways, invisible. But I didn't realize how much this would affect my professional journey until much later. It wasn't just the fact that I didn't see people who looked like me—it was the absence of diverse perspectives that made the environment feel restrictive and limiting.

You see, as I look back now, I realize that diversity isn't just a nice thing to have. It's essential for any organization that wants to thrive. **Different perspectives bring innovation, creativity, and a deeper understanding of consumer needs.** A lack of diversity leads to a narrow worldview, and unfortunately, that narrowness was something I felt on a daily basis.

Despite these feelings of isolation, I stayed focused on the work. I focused on the marketing campaigns, on the travel opportunities, and on making a name for myself. But deep down, there was a voice—an uncomfortable, nagging voice—that kept asking, *What about me? What about my voice, my unique perspective, and the richness of my culture?*

At that time, I didn't know how to answer it. I had been taught to remain silent in spaces where I felt different. To be grateful. To not rock the boat. To just "play the game." But what I didn't know was that this was the first step toward living in a **scarcity mindset**—one that held me back from speaking my truth and sharing my unique perspective.

> **My silence was the very thing holding me back.**

The Meeting That Changed Everything

It was four months into my role when I found myself in a meeting with the CEO of the company. We were discussing a new

Audacious

menu change that would affect the Atlanta and Houston markets. As the marketing manager, I was in the room to observe, take notes, and provide feedback if I had something truly valuable to contribute. At the time, I wasn't sure that I did.

I was still in my late twenties, still finding my voice, still in that awkward phase of trying to figure out where I fit in this new corporate world. I had always been taught that, as a Black woman, I needed to be careful not to "ruffle feathers"—to be grateful for every opportunity, even when it didn't feel right. I was "lucky to be here."

But then, during the meeting, the CEO made a statement that shattered the illusion of my "dream job."

He said, "Let's take the chicken and waffles off the menu. It's bringing in too many Black people to the restaurant."

My mind went blank. Was he really saying that? Did I hear him right? **He continued, "They don't tip, and we don't want them here."**

I froze. I wanted to scream. I wanted to stand up, shout, and tell him how deeply offensive and hurtful those words were. But I didn't. I remained silent. I sat there, in complete disbelief, absorbing the weight of what he was saying. And in that moment, I realized something about myself that I wasn't ready to face: I had allowed fear to silence me.

I had been conditioned to a mindset of scarcity, believing that speaking up—challenging him—could cost me my job, my career, everything I had worked for. I had been taught to stay silent, to be "grateful," to never rock the boat. But in doing so, I had buried my truth. And this wasn't just about a job. This was about courage. This was about my race, my culture, and the weight of an assumption—that Black people didn't tip—that made me feel, at my core, that he believed we weren't worthy. And that was something I could no longer ignore.

Looking back now, I wish I had said something. I wish I had stood up for my community, for my culture, and for myself. But I didn't know then that my silence was the very thing holding me back.

This moment was the catalyst that would eventually force me to confront my own scarcity mindset. I had been living my life with the belief that there was "not enough" to go around. Not enough space for my voice. Not enough room for my ideas. Not enough opportunity for me to take up space and make an impact. But at that moment, I realized that the scarcity I was living in was not just about my career—it was about how I saw the world.

The Scarcity Mindset: Living in Fear

The scarcity mindset is something that many of us live with, even if we don't realize it. It's the belief that there are only so many resources to go around—that opportunities are limited, and if someone else gets something, it means there's less for you. It's the fear that if you speak up, you might lose your job, your relationships, or your security.

This is the mentality that says, "There's not enough money, not enough time, not enough love, and not enough opportunities to go around." This belief permeates every aspect of life, shaping how you think, feel, and act. It's like wearing tinted glasses that cast a shadow of limitation on everything you see. It keeps you stuck in a place of fear, stress, and competition, where you're constantly worried that if you don't act quickly, you'll miss out on the one chance you have.

Audacious

When I was in that meeting with the CEO, I was living in that mindset. I was afraid that speaking up would jeopardize my place at the table. I feared that challenging him would cause me to lose the job I had fought so hard to get. I was stuck in a place of limited thinking, believing that there was only so much room for me to succeed.

What I didn't realize was that the scarcity mindset was not just preventing me from speaking up—it was preventing me from growing. It was keeping me small, keeping me in a place where I couldn't see beyond the fear of losing what I already had. Scarcity breeds fear and uncertainty, while abundance opens up a world of possibilities.

> **Scarcity breeds fear and uncertainty, while abundance opens up a world of possibilities.**

Understanding the Scarcity Mindset and Limiting Beliefs

Scarcity sneaks in uninvited and overstays its welcome. It plants itself in your mind, making itself comfortable in your thoughts, your habits, and your choices. It convinces you that there isn't enough—enough love, success, time, or resources—and keeps you from seeing the abundance that already exists in your life. Scarcity shows up in all forms and through all people, no matter what your role may be. Here are some ways scarcity can show up in our mindsets:

As a Mom
Scarcity can manifest as guilt and fear of not being enough for your children. You might constantly compare yourself to other moms—wondering if you're spending enough time with your kids, providing the best opportunities, or creating the perfect

home environment. Scarcity whispers that you're falling short, that you're not giving your family everything they deserve, even when you're doing your absolute best.

As a College Student
In college, scarcity can look like an overwhelming fear of missing out (FOMO). You might feel like you're not taking enough classes, joining enough organizations, or making the right connections to set yourself up for future success. It can make you overextend yourself, trying to do everything while still feeling like you're falling behind your peers.

As a Single Person
For singles, scarcity can show up as the belief that you're running out of time to find "the one" or build a meaningful relationship. You might look at friends who are married or in long-term relationships and feel like love is a resource in short supply—and somehow, you're being left out.

Scarcity makes you focus on what you lack—skills, connections, or recognition—rather than celebrating how far you've come. Often, the roots of scarcity can be traced back to childhood experiences, cultural moments, and even failures that have shaped how you see the world. Perhaps you grew up in an environment where resources were limited, and the narrative was always about survival rather than thriving. Maybe societal pressures or cultural norms instilled a sense of competition, making it feel like success is a finite resource. Or perhaps past failures left you hesitant to dream big, reinforcing the fear that abundance is out of reach.

> Abundance is not a destination—it's a mindset.

But here's the truth: Abundance is not a destination—it's a mindset. And shifting from scarcity to abundance requires intentionality and practice. It begins with recognizing the moments when scarcity shows up in your thoughts and challenging them. Instead of focusing on what you lack, reflect on what you've already accomplished, the strengths you bring to the table, and the opportunities that are still ahead.

The Shift: Embracing Abundance

After I left that company, I had a lot of time to reflect on my experiences there. I spent hours journaling and thinking about what had gone wrong, what I had learned, and where I wanted to go next. Slowly, I began to realize that the biggest barrier to my success wasn't the company, the industry, or even the people around me. It was my own mindset.

I had been operating from a place of scarcity for so long that I didn't know what abundance looked like. **An abundance mindset isn't just about having more money, more success, or more things—it's about believing that there's more than enough for everyone.** It's about trusting that opportunities will come, even if one door closes. It's about knowing that your voice matters and that your unique perspective is valuable.

Here are some key characteristics of the abundance mindset: it's about seeing opportunities where others see obstacles, celebrating others' successes without feeling threatened, and trusting that there is more than enough to go around. An abundance mindset encourages gratitude, resilience, and the belief that your potential is limitless.

Shifting from Scarcity to Abundance

While we are talking about abundance, it's important to clarify what an abundance mindset is not. It's not about ignoring challenges or pretending everything is perfect. It's not reckless optimism or a denial of reality—it's a balanced, intentional way of viewing the world with hope, gratitude, and possibility.

When you shift from scarcity to abundance, you stop seeing the world as a place of competition. You start seeing it as a place of collaboration. You stop fearing failure and start seeing it as an opportunity to grow.

Abundance is about trusting that the world is limitless. It's about believing that you have the power to create your own opportunities. You stop measuring your worth based on what you don't have and start embracing what you do have. **You become the creator of your own reality.**

> When you shift from scarcity to abundance, you stop seeing the world as a place of competition. You start seeing it as a place of collaboration. You stop fearing failure and start seeing it as an opportunity to grow.

The Family Crisis: Scarcity Versus Abundance at Home

The real test of my abundance mindset came when my husband and I had our twins. Suddenly, the pressures of parenthood, work, and finances collided, and we found ourselves in a difficult situation where we needed the twins to give us space to work and think. The cost of day care was astronomical, and it felt impossible to cover tuition for three young kids while caring for them and balancing my work-from-home schedule. We were stuck in a scarcity mindset again.

We made a decision to find a solution. We met with a coach to help us navigate our challenge, and one of the first things she asked was, "What is your current distraction?" Without hesitation, we both answered the same way: "Having the twins at home." Our older child was in school part of the time, but the twins were not. We loved our children deeply, but balancing work, life, and parenting the twins in the same space was overwhelming.

The coach listened, then asked, "What would it take to change that?" We glanced at each other, both thinking the same thing but too hesitant to say it out loud. Day care. We both knew that putting our kids in day care would allow us the focus and space we desperately needed, but the cost felt impossible. How could we really afford to send three kids to day care?

For about a week, we wrestled with the numbers. Every calculation seemed to confirm our fears—it was too expensive, too much of a stretch. But then the coach challenged us: "What if you shifted your mindset? What if you believed that investing in this change would create more opportunities for abundance in your life?" That question hit me like a ton of bricks. The cost of inaction was far greater than the cost of investing in a solution. We would be faced with losing business, not gaining more clients, and ultimately our business failing if we did not make the shift. We could choose to stay in the same place, stuck in our fears, or we could embrace the possibility of change and move forward with confidence.

It wasn't easy, but we began to shift. Instead of focusing on what it was costing us, we thought about what this choice could unlock—more productivity, more energy, more focus, and ultimately, more growth for our family. We sat down, crunched the numbers one more time, and decided to take a leap of faith. We shifted our scarcity mindset to one of abundance and belief.

Making that decision wasn't just about finances—it was about trusting that by investing in ourselves and our family, we were creating the space for something greater. And looking back, it was one of the best decisions we've ever made. As a result, I now look at numbers and math in a whole new light.

The Audacity Equation

The new math is audacious math. Audacious math operates on a simple yet transformative formula:

> The cost of inaction was far greater than the cost of investing in a solution.

The Formula Is Mindset + Affirmation = Action

This equation encapsulates what it takes to move from thought to bold, meaningful action. It begins with your mindset—the foundation upon which every decision and behavior is built. If your mindset is rooted in scarcity, it creates self-imposed limitations, shrinking your belief in what's possible. On the other hand, an abundance mindset fuels confidence, creativity, and audacity. A 2023 mindset survey by the Think To DO Institute (retrieved from thinktodoinstitute.com) found that individuals with a "Growth Abundance" mindset reported a mean positive life outcome score of 4.1, compared to 3.1 for those with a "Fixed Scarcity" mindset. This suggests that adopting an abundance mindset is associated with enhanced well-being and positive life outcomes.

Affirmation is more than just positive thinking; it is a deliberate practice of shaping your internal narrative. By consistently affirming empowering beliefs, you cultivate a mindset that aligns with growth, resilience, and possibility. These affirmations serve as mental anchors, reinforcing confidence and redirecting focus toward opportunities rather than limitations. When repeated with conviction, they shift subconscious patterns, replacing doubt with determination. This transformation lays the foundation for meaningful action—action driven not by fear, but by a deep-seated belief in potential and abundance.

Affirmation acts as the bridge between mindset and action. It reinforces belief, reprogramming the stories you tell yourself about what's achievable. When mindset and affirmation work in harmony, they lead to action that defies boundaries—the kind of action that can only be described as audacious.

Examples of the Audacity Equation in Action

- In Career: A scarcity mindset says, *I'm not qualified enough to apply for this role*. But with an abundance mindset and affirmations like *I bring unique strengths and experience to the table*, you take bold action and apply anyway—often opening doors you didn't expect.
- In Personal Finance: A scarcity mindset tells you, *I can't afford to invest in myself*, whether it's education, childcare, or a business opportunity. But shifting to abundance and affirming, you begin thinking, *Investing in myself today will lead to greater returns tomorrow*. This empowers you to make decisions that create long-term growth.
- In Relationships: Scarcity whispers, *I'm not worthy of love or support*, while abundance affirms, *I am deserving of connection and belonging*. This shift allows you to pursue and nurture meaningful

relationships instead of settling for less or isolating yourself.

Here's what I've learned: **Abundance is a choice.** You can choose to believe in scarcity, or you can choose to believe in the abundance that life has to offer.

Every day, you have the opportunity to step into a mindset of abundance. Whether it's in your career, your relationships, or your finances, you get to decide how you see the world. You can choose fear and doubt, or you can choose possibility and growth.

If you're stuck in a mindset of scarcity, it's time to shift. Start by imagining a life of abundance. See the opportunities, not the limitations. Know that there's enough for you and everyone around you.

Strategies for Shifting from Scarcity to an Abundance Mindset

Strategy #1: Imagine a Life of Abundance
Explanation: When you imagine abundance, you're training your mind to see beyond your current limitations. This visualization shifts your focus from *what you don't have* to *what's possible*, reinforcing the mindset component of the audacious math formula.

Application: Take a moment to envision what your life could look like if you believed abundance was limitless. What opportunities would you pursue? How would you show up for yourself and others? This exercise helps you expand your perspective and opens your mind to bold possibilities.

Audacious

Strategy #2: See the Opportunities, Not the Limitations
Explanation: Opportunities often hide behind obstacles. By choosing to see opportunities, you strengthen your mindset and cultivate a sense of abundance. This perspective leads to affirmations of possibility and bold action.
Application: In every challenge, actively look for the opportunity. Ask yourself, *What can I learn here? How can this situation help me grow?* This simple question shifts your perspective.

Strategy #3: Use Affirmations of Abundance and Possibility
Explanation: Affirmations strengthen belief by replacing scarcity-focused thoughts with empowering ones. They connect mindset to action, making audacious math come alive in your everyday decisions.
Application: Repeat affirmations like *I am capable of achieving my goals* or *there is always enough to meet my needs*. Write them down and say them aloud daily.

By practicing these strategies, you align your mindset, affirmations, and actions, ensuring that you consistently show up with audacity and a belief in abundance. This isn't just a one-time shift; it's a daily commitment to thinking bigger, dreaming bolder, and acting as though the life you desire is already within your grasp.

The stories we tell ourselves become the realities we live. Scarcity thoughts whisper limits into your mind, convincing you that what you have is all there will ever be. If you believe you can't afford cable TV, then that belief becomes your truth. But abundance thoughts flip the script—they invite possibility, opportunity, and growth. When you dare to believe that a

Shifting from Scarcity to Abundance

million dollars, a thriving life, or boundless opportunities are within your reach, you open the door for them to become your reality. The difference isn't in your resources; it's in your mindset. Scarcity confines you; abundance frees you. Choose abundance. Rewrite your story. Live a life without limits and watch as doors you never imagined swing wide open.

CHAPTER 6

The Audacity of Authenticity

WHAT IF THE KEY to a fulfilling life isn't found in fitting in but in standing out? In a world that often celebrates conformity, being authentic can feel like an act of rebellion. We live in a time when the pressure to fit in, to adhere to societal norms, and to meet the expectations of others can be suffocating. Social media presents curated versions of life, workplaces demand professionalism that often feels detached from humanity, and personal relationships can become arenas where we hide parts of ourselves to gain acceptance. This constant tug to conform takes a toll: It chips away at our sense of self, leaving us disconnected from who we truly are and what we truly want.

What if the answer to overcoming the pressure of posturing lies in embracing our authenticity—in showing up as the truest, most honest version of ourselves? Authenticity is not just a buzzword; it's a powerful principle. It's about being true to yourself, your values, and your beliefs. It's about rejecting the mask of conformity and stepping boldly into the world as yourself.

Authenticity as an Act of Audacity

Embracing authenticity is not for the faint of heart. It's an audacious act because it requires courage—the courage to be vulnerable, to risk rejection, and to stand firm in your truth even when it challenges the status quo. Authenticity means saying, "This is who I am," even when you fear judgment. It means holding on to your values when it would be easier to follow the crowd. It means pursuing what aligns with your true self, even if it defies societal expectations.

Authenticity and audacity are inseparable. Being authentic is inherently audacious because it challenges the narrative that we must be something other than ourselves to be successful, accepted, or loved. It says, "I'm enough just as I am, and I'm not afraid to show it." When you choose authenticity, you are choosing to disrupt the patterns of conformity that keep so many people stuck. You are choosing to live a life that is uniquely and unapologetically yours.

> Being authentic is inherently audacious because it challenges the narrative that we must be something other than ourselves to be successful, accepted, or loved.

Authenticity isn't just about self-expression; it's about alignment. When you align your actions with your values and your decisions with your beliefs, you create a life that feels meaningful and satisfying. But authenticity doesn't just transform your inner world; it also transforms the way the world responds to you. Authenticity attracts opportunities, builds genuine connections, and establishes trust. People are drawn to those who are real, and opportunities flow to those who stand confidently in their truth. How can you harness this power in your own life? Let's find out. The following pages offer a roadmap to embracing the authenticity that will lead you to a more fulfilling life and career.

The Toll of Conformity

Before we dive into how to embrace authenticity, it's important to acknowledge what's at stake when we don't. Conformity may bring temporary comfort—the safety of fitting in, the approval of others—but it comes at a cost. When we hide parts of ourselves to please others, we lose the opportunity to connect with people who would truly value us for who we are. When we pursue careers or goals that don't align with our values, we may achieve success, but it will feel hollow. And when we silence our true selves, we rob the world of the unique perspective and talents only we can offer.

The cost of conformity is high: burnout, dissatisfaction, and a lingering sense of "Is this all there is?" In fact, research shows stress and burnout are prevalent issues with significant consequences that impact health and other diseases that could ultimately arise.

Living authentically isn't always the easiest path, but it's the only path that leads to genuine fulfillment. I know firsthand the negative impact of conformity and shame, guilt and imposter syndrome.

The Cost of Conformity: A Lesson in Authenticity

When I think back to my last corporate gig, the first word that comes to mind is *misaligned*. From the moment I stepped into that role, I felt like a fish out of water, constantly trying to shape myself into someone I wasn't just to fit in. It was an environment where authenticity wasn't valued—only assimilation.

Before my long-awaited vacation, I got box braids—low-maintenance, protective, and perfect for the trip. They made me feel free, confident, and effortlessly myself. But as my return to work approached, that confidence started to waver.

I wasn't worried about catching up on emails or jumping back into meetings—I was worried about **my hair**.

I knew the questions were coming:

"Wow, your hair looks so different! How does it work?"

"Did you do it yourself?"

"How long does it last?"

Questions that weren't just about curiosity, but about difference. About standing out in a space where I was already conscious of how I showed up.

And that's when it hit me—if I felt uncomfortable bringing my full self to work, was this a space truly meant for me?

That moment was a turning point. It wasn't just about hair; it was about **authenticity**. If I had to shrink, conform, or second-guess how I presented myself just to avoid scrutiny, then I wasn't in a place that valued me for who I truly was.

I realized then: I deserve to be in spaces where I don't have to explain, justify, or tone down any part of myself. Where I can show up as me—bold, unapologetic, and fully present.

The Audacity of Authenticity

If you recall from the last chapter, I was the only Black woman working at the company, and I felt alone, invisible, and unseen. I felt that I wasn't accepted for who I was, and that persistent dissonance weighed heavily on me, both professionally and personally.

One particular incident stands out as the turning point. I was working on a major project with the entire marketing team, tasked with reviewing and signing off on marketing materials. It was a straightforward responsibility, but amidst the stress of masking my true self and navigating the unspoken demands to conform, I missed a spelling error. The materials were printed and shipped to five hundred stores before the mistake was caught.

The fallout was immediate and brutal. The team's reaction was less about the error and more about assigning blame. Their ridicule wasn't just harsh; it was isolating. I felt abandoned in a way I hadn't experienced before—a profound loneliness that underscored how out of place I truly was. Their words and actions made it clear: I wasn't one of them. I didn't belong.

But here's the thing—looking back, I realize that the mistake wasn't just about a missed spelling error. Yes, it did impact the company's reputation for excellence, but the pressure of the environment made me believe that mistakes could not be tolerated and it was not a safe space to be authentically me. It was the inevitable result of trying to conform to an environment that demanded I leave my authentic self at the door. The constant pressure to pretend, to suppress my instincts and ideas, created a tension that made me second-guess everything. I wasn't just doing a job; I was performing a version of myself that wasn't real. And it was exhausting.

That environment didn't foster collaboration or growth; it fed on fear and perfectionism. Every day, I felt I had to prove myself in ways that didn't align with my values or strengths. I had to fight to be heard, to be seen, and to feel like I mattered. Over time, that effort chipped away at my confidence, making the mistake—and the ridicule that followed—almost inevitable.

In the end, it wasn't the mistake that made me leave; it was the realization that I could no longer deny my own truth. My truth was finding a space where I could show up authentically as myself. The buildup of feeling like I couldn't be that way was too much. The toxic culture and leadership weren't just a mismatch—they were a mirror reflecting a version of myself back at me that I didn't want to become.

Walking away wasn't easy, but it was necessary. That experience taught me a powerful lesson: When you suppress your authentic self to fit into a space that doesn't value who you are, you're bound to stumble. And when you do, those same spaces will often leave you to pick up the pieces alone.

Now, I approach every opportunity with a renewed commitment to authenticity. I know that the right environment will value my ideas, my contributions, and most importantly, *me*. Because when you can show up as yourself, the work isn't just better—it's meaningful. Maybe you've felt like this before and found yourself in some spaces where you can't be your authentic self. I want to share with you some steps to walking out your truth audaciously.

> **When you suppress your authentic self to fit into a space that doesn't value who you are, you're bound to stumble.**

Steps to Embrace Authenticity as Your Superpower

1. Know Yourself
The first step to living authentically is understanding who you are. Take time to reflect on your values, beliefs, and passions. What matters most to you? What do you stand for? What makes you come alive? Knowing yourself is the foundation of authenticity.

2. Define Your Boundaries
Authenticity requires boundaries. It's about knowing where you end and others begin. Be clear about what you will and won't tolerate. Protect your time, energy, and values from anything that threatens to pull you out of alignment.

3. Practice Vulnerability
Being authentic means being real, and being real means being vulnerable. It's okay to admit when you don't have all the answers, to share your struggles, and to express your true emotions. Vulnerability isn't a weakness; it's a strength that fosters deeper connections.

4. Take Audacious Action
Authenticity requires action. It's not enough to know your truth; you have to live it. Make decisions that align with your values, pursue goals that reflect your passions, and show up as your true self in every space you occupy.

5. Silence the Noise
Not everyone will understand or support your authenticity, and that's okay. Silence the external noise of judgment

and comparison, and trust the internal voice that guides you. Remember, your authenticity is not up for debate.

The Rewards of Authenticity: Opening Doors to Opportunity

Authenticity isn't just about being yourself—it's about reclaiming your power and stepping fully into your truth. When you stop trying to conform and start showing up as your authentic self, the world begins to respond in unexpected and remarkable ways. For me, embracing authenticity transformed every part of my life, bringing greater confidence, deeper relationships, and opportunities I never thought possible. It has been a journey, but the rewards have been undeniable. Here are some of the rewards that await you when you step into your authentic self:

- **Increased Confidence and Self-Esteem:** Owning my story gave me the strength to walk into any room without shrinking. I no longer questioned my place or my worth.
- **Stronger Relationships:** Vulnerability became the bridge to real, meaningful connections with others.
- **Greater Opportunities:** By being myself, I attracted opportunities that aligned with my values and purpose.
- **A Sense of Fulfillment:** I found joy in knowing that the life I'm building is rooted in truth, not in what others expect of me.

One of the most powerful examples of a time when showing up as my authentic self paid off professionally was the journey

The Audacity of Authenticity

to my book deal—a moment when authenticity opened a door I never anticipated.

The Power of Vulnerability: From a Call to a Book Deal

It started innocently enough—a routine call with a potential client, someone I had been eager to work with. We exchanged the usual pleasantries, and then she asked, "Where are you from?" A simple, casual question, but one that unknowingly sparked a turning point.

"Murfreesboro, Tennessee," I replied.

Her response caught me off guard. "No way! I live in Murfreesboro!"

In that moment, something shifted. Sharing a hometown felt serendipitous, almost like a nudge from the universe to go deeper. When she asked where in Murfreesboro I had grown up, I had a choice: Keep the conversation light or take a risk by opening up.

I chose to be honest. "I didn't grow up on the side of Murfreesboro you might imagine," I said. "My story comes from the overlooked corners of town."

What followed was one of the most meaningful conversations of my life. I shared how being one of the first biracial kids in Murfreesboro shaped my experience—navigating both the challenges of being Black and the privilege I observed but didn't share. I talked about my two grandmothers, whose stories reflected both the opportunities and inequities that shaped my family's history. My white grandmother, who worked as the mayor's secretary, bought fifty-eight acres of land in the 1950s, creating a legacy for her children. My Black grandmother, brilliant and hardworking, was the valedictorian of her class but spent her life managing a factory and left behind only an insurance policy for her family.

These stories weren't easy to share, but they were real. They were *me*. And as I spoke, I felt the weight of the masks I'd worn for years fall away. For the first time in my professional life, I wasn't trying to "fit in." I wasn't curating or editing my story to make it more palatable. I was showing up, fully and authentically.

What happened next was nothing short of transformative. The woman on the other end of the call didn't judge or dismiss me. She leaned in. She understood. She saw me—not just as a professional, but as a person with depth, complexity, and a unique perspective.

The connection we forged during that call led to a collaboration, but it also led to something far greater: the opportunity to share my story on a larger platform. That conversation planted the seed for my book deal, an opportunity I could never have imagined if I hadn't embraced my authenticity.

This experience was a stark contrast to my time at the corporate job I'd left. Back then, I believed that hiding parts of myself was necessary to survive. I tried to conform, to blend in, to be who I thought they wanted me to be—and it drained me, leading to mistakes, isolation, and ultimately, resignation.

But on that call, when I allowed myself to be vulnerable and authentic, the results were the opposite. Instead of rejection, I found acceptance. Instead of judgment, I found understanding. And instead of limitation, I found an opportunity that aligned with my purpose.

The Power of Authenticity: What Happens When You Show Up as Yourself

When you embrace who you are, the world begins to respond. You attract relationships, opportunities, and experiences that honor your truth. And you begin to realize that the stories you thought made you "different" are the very things that make you valuable.

My journey isn't unique—it's a reminder for anyone feeling stuck in environments that don't honor their authenticity. When you let go of the need to conform and step into your truth, the rewards are transformative. Whether it's increased confidence, stronger relationships, or opportunities you never dreamed of, the power of authenticity is undeniable.

If there's one thing I've learned, it's this: Your story matters. When you embrace it, you open doors—not just for yourself, but for others who need the space to be authentic too.

I've seen this truth play out up close and personal in the lives of two women I know—Jessica and Nicole. They went through incredible transformations in their professional lives, and their story offers a powerful lesson on the value of authenticity. The lesson is this: The true measure of success isn't in the deals we close, the titles we hold, or the goals we achieve. True success is in letting go of the need to impress and instead, fully embracing who we are. As I share their story, consider where you

> **The true measure of success isn't in the deals we close, the titles we hold, or the goals we achieve. True success is in letting go of the need to impress and instead, fully embracing who we are.**

are in your relation to living an authentic life. These lessons are not just for business leaders or entrepreneurs—they're for anyone trying to find deeper, more meaningful connections in their personal and professional life. I hope you can see something of yourself in their story.

Jessica's Struggle: The Pressure to Fit In

Jessica was the kind of person who could light up a room with her kindness. She had a way of making people feel comfortable, heard, and valued. Her friends and colleagues often described her as someone whose energy felt like "home." But despite this natural gift, Jessica began to feel the weight of an unspoken pressure in her industry—the pressure to be more than just warm, more than just kind, more than just a "people person."

In the fast-paced, cutthroat world of business, she watched others navigate spaces with effortless confidence. People seemed to have their pitches down to a science, their networking strategies on point, and their social media personas carefully curated. Jessica, by contrast, felt like she was stumbling through every event and every conversation. She began to doubt whether her heartfelt approach was enough in a world that seemed to reward boldness over empathy.

Trying to fit in, Jessica started mimicking what she saw in others. She rehearsed introductions, focused on meeting as many people as possible, and adopted a stiffer, less natural demeanor. But despite all her efforts, she felt disconnected. Her interactions became shallow and transactional, and she missed the deep, meaningful conversations that left people feeling truly seen.

The Audacity of Authenticity

The more she tried to fit in, the more she realized she was losing herself.

Nicole's Struggle: The Mask of Perfection

Nicole's journey was different but rooted in the same fear of inadequacy. From the outside, Nicole seemed polished, ambitious, and in control. She was a leader others admired, someone who appeared to have it all together. But behind the scenes, Nicole was haunted by the fear that vulnerability would expose her weaknesses.

For Nicole, success meant perfection. She was always on, always poised, and always in control of every interaction. Her professional life had become a performance. Every meeting, every event, every handshake was carefully choreographed. But the more she perfected the act, the more exhausted she became. Her relationships felt hollow, and she realized people only knew the version of her she allowed them to see—not the real Nicole.

Deep down, she longed to let people in, but fear held her back. Vulnerability felt like a risk she couldn't afford to take.

The Fateful Encounter: Where Authenticity Shifts the Tide

Jessica and Nicole met at a networking event, a space neither wanted to be in. Jessica stood quietly on the sidelines, her calm energy a stark contrast to the bustling room of people vying for attention. Intrigued, Nicole approached her, drawn to something she couldn't quite put her finger on.

Their conversation was unlike anything Nicole had experienced in similar settings. Jessica wasn't trying to impress or control the dialogue; she was simply present. As they talked, Nicole found herself opening up, sharing the doubts and insecurities she had spent years hiding.

"I feel like I'm always performing," Nicole admitted. "I want to be real with people, but I'm scared it'll make me seem weak."

Jessica smiled knowingly. "I get it," she said. "I used to think the same thing. But I've learned that people connect with you when you're real. Vulnerability isn't weakness—it's strength. It's what allows people to see who you really are, and that's when the magic happens."

Their conversation was a turning point. For Nicole, it was the first time she felt free to be honest about her struggles. And for Jessica, it was a reminder of the power of authenticity—not just for herself, but for the people she connected with.

Letting Go of Control: The Courage to Be Authentic

After their conversation, Nicole decided to let go of the perfection she had clung to for so long. In her next business meeting, she allowed herself to be present rather than rehearsed. She asked questions from genuine curiosity, shared her insights without overthinking them, and let pauses in the conversation happen naturally. The results were transformative. People responded to her differently, drawn to her openness and sincerity. Her connections deepened, and for the first time in years, she felt seen—not for her accomplishments, but for who she truly was.

Jessica, meanwhile, continued to lean into her natural gifts. She stopped trying to emulate others and trusted in her ability to connect deeply and authentically. Her quiet strength and empathetic nature became her unique advantage in a noisy, competitive world.

The Power of Showing Up Authentically

Jessica and Nicole's journeys underscore a powerful truth: The greatest success comes when we stop trying to be who the world expects us to be and start embracing who we truly are. Authenticity isn't just about being honest with others—it's about being honest with ourselves. It's about trusting that our unique qualities are not just enough—they're exactly what the world needs.

When you show up authentically, you attract the right opportunities, the right relationships, and the right spaces where you can thrive. You create a foundation for a life and career that is fulfilling, not because it's perfect, but because it's real.

The Audacious Act of Authenticity

It takes courage to be different, to stand out, and to be true to yourself—especially in a world that pressures us to conform. And that's why authenticity is an inherently audacious act. It's choosing to embrace your strengths, your quirks, and even your vulnerabilities in a society that often equates worth with perfection.

When you show up as yourself, you open the door to deeper relationships, greater opportunities, and a sense of purpose that comes from living in alignment with who you truly are. You're more likely to take risks, pursue your passions, and live a life that feels meaningful and fulfilling.

Audacious

So here's my challenge to you: Be audaciously authentic. Trust that your story, your voice, and your unique perspective matter. When you let go of the need to impress and instead focus on connecting, you'll discover that authenticity will lead you to the spaces where you truly belong.

The world doesn't need another polished façade. It needs *you*. Show up, be real, and watch the magic unfold.

CHAPTER 7

Stay True to Your "Why," Even When It's Hard

AUDACITY WITHOUT PURPOSE IS like a rocket without a guidance system—it might launch with incredible force and energy, but without a clear direction, it risks veering off course, or worse, failing to reach its destination. Purpose is the invisible thread that weaves meaning into our actions, aligning them with something greater than ourselves. It is the driving force behind perseverance, the quiet strength that pushes us forward when obstacles arise and the excitement of new beginnings wears thin.

Purpose is more than a lofty goal or a business plan. It's a deeply held value, a force that motivates and sustains action, even in the face of difficulty. It isn't confined to our careers or businesses; it touches every area of our lives. Purpose is what gives us the courage to dream big, the patience to endure setbacks, and the determination to see things through. It is the "why" that makes the "what" and "how" worthwhile.

A strong sense of purpose doesn't mean life will be easy. In fact, purpose often calls us to walk harder paths, to take bigger risks, and to pursue dreams that might seem impossible. But it also gives us the strength to persevere, the clarity to make decisions, and the resilience to bounce back when we falter. This was key to me walking my own purpose journey and discovering my "why."

Purpose-Driven Perseverance: My Audacious Journey

When I was a little girl, I dreamed of being a fashion designer. I would dress up in anything I could find—church dresses, ruffled socks, old scarves—and transform them into bold and creative ensembles. I layered tops, added accessories, and always topped things off with a stylish hat. Every time I pieced together a new look, I imagined myself on a grand stage, my designs captivating an adoring audience. So when family members asked, "What do you want to be when you grow up?" I always responded with conviction: "A fashion designer."

But as I grew older, the world began to dim the light of that dream. People said things like "It's a tough field" or "Fashion doesn't make money." They suggested practical careers like medicine or law—fields they thought would ensure stability. Yet, the thought of a life spent disconnected from my creativity was unbearable. Slowly, though, I began to believe the doubts of others. Maybe, I thought, my dream wasn't meant to be.

When college applications rolled around, none of the schools I was accepted into offered fashion merchandising. I convinced myself that maybe fashion wasn't in the cards for me and pivoted to majoring in interior design with a focus on architecture. At first, it felt like a compromise, but the creative possibilities within the field surprised me. Growing up in small apartments, I had never imagined the artistry behind designing spaces. Still, even as I immersed myself in my studies, that childhood dream of fashion lingered in the background.

During my senior year, while completing internship hours, fate stepped in. One day, while grocery shopping, I came across a magazine featuring a fellow alumna who had achieved my dream—she was a fashion merchandiser for Ralph Lauren. It reignited a spark I thought had long faded. She helped connect me with Kimora Lee Simmons's team at Baby Phat, and soon I was offered an internship in fashion. My childhood dream was within reach. But the choice wasn't simple: Pursuing the internship meant abandoning the practical path I had worked so hard to complete. In the end, I chose to fulfill the degree requirements, leaving fashion behind yet again.

That decision stayed with me, haunting me at times with the question of "what if?" But life has a way of bringing things full circle.

Rediscovering My "Why" Through Motherhood

Fifteen years later, motherhood would lead me back to the purpose I had left behind. After a harrowing thirty-five days in the NICU with my daughter, I emerged transformed. Those days shaped my understanding of resilience and advocacy. I wanted my daughter to grow up knowing that she could dream big, that she was seen and celebrated. A few months after bringing her home, I went to Target, searching for clothing that reflected her—a beautiful brown girl with radiant skin and big, confident hair. But as I combed the shelves, my heart sank. There were no characters, no designs, no products that looked like her.

That moment changed everything. **I realized I couldn't wait for someone else to create what I was looking for.** If I wanted my daughter—and other children like her—to feel represented, I had to build it myself. And just like that, the dream I thought I had left behind came rushing back. My childhood passion for fashion wasn't gone; it had been waiting for this exact moment.

The Roadblocks to Representation

I launched Elle Olivia as an online e-commerce brand in February 2022 with the goal of becoming a household name in children's fashion. My vision was simple yet profound: to create a lifestyle brand that embodied representation, diversity, and boundless possibilities for all children. I wanted every child of color to see themselves reflected and celebrated in the products on store shelves.

From the very beginning, I had always dreamed of seeing my brand on the shelves of Target. Growing up, Target was more than just a store—it was a symbol of possibility, a place where dreams felt just within reach. So when we launched our brand, I knew I had to aim high.

Six months after launching my brand, I decided to take a bold step. I sent a cold pitch email to Target. In that email, I shared my observations about the gaps I saw in the baby and toddler market. There weren't enough options that truly celebrated diversity and representation in a way that resonated with moms like me—moms who wanted their daughters to feel seen, celebrated, and inspired to dream big. I explained how

Stay True to Your "Why," Even When It's Hard

my line of pajamas and clothing wasn't just about comfort or style—it was about creating pieces that told a story of possibility, representation, and joy.

To my amazement, that email opened the door to an opportunity that I could have only imagined before. When Target gave us the incredible opportunity to debut our pajama collection in four hundred stores, the excitement was almost overwhelming. But as the reality of scaling a brand set in, so did the challenges. What I thought was an initial order of ten thousand units turned out to be seventy thousand units. The cost was astronomical, and I had to pay to produce the clothing myself. I wouldn't get paid by Target until they received the clothes. As a first-time producer, I quickly realized that securing funding would be my greatest obstacle.

Traditional financing, it quickly became clear, wasn't an option. Lenders saw me as high-risk. Each rejection felt like a punch to the gut. But through every "no," I clung to my "why"—the image of children seeing themselves represented kept me going. This wasn't just about launching a product; it was about making a statement. I wasn't doing this for myself—I was doing it for them.

Desperate to meet the financial demands of production, I turned to alternative funding sources. One funder finally said yes, but their terms were steep. I signed, believing it was my only option, but soon realized the cost was far greater than I had anticipated. The loan's interest ballooned, and I found myself trapped in mounting debt and paralyzed by the fears I mentioned in Chapter 1. I vividly remember sitting on my bathroom floor, consumed by regret and disbelief. How had I allowed myself to get here?

But even in my lowest moments, my purpose wouldn't let me quit. I reminded myself of why I had started—to give children what I hadn't found for my daughter. My "why" gave me the strength to navigate the debt, fulfill the orders, and continue building my dream.

In October 2022, our pajama line debuted in Target stores nationwide. Seeing Elle Olivia on those shelves was surreal. It wasn't just a personal victory—it was proof that representation matters and perseverance pays off. I imagined the smiles of little girls picking up our products and seeing themselves reflected. That image made every sleepless night, every financial hurdle, and every moment of doubt worth it.

The journey to Elle Olivia taught me that purpose-driven perseverance is unstoppable. When your "why" is clear, it becomes the fuel that sustains you through challenges. Obstacles will come, and the road may twist and turn, but purpose is the anchor that keeps you grounded.

For me, the dream wasn't just about creating a brand; it was about creating representation. And that vision kept me fighting, even when the odds felt insurmountable. Dreams aren't easy, but when they're rooted in your "why"—the ultimate purpose behind your vision—they're always worth the fight.

Discovering Your "Why": Beyond the What and the How

Many of us know *what* we do. Some of us can articulate *how* we do it. But far fewer of us have taken the time to define *why* we do it. And yet, the "why" is the most important of the three. It's the foundation on which everything else is built. Let me give you a deeper understanding of the difference between each.

- **The "What":** These are the tangible aspects of your life—your job, your hobbies, your daily activities. For example, "I create children's clothing."
- **The "How":** This is the method or approach you use to do what you do. For instance, "I design inclusive, representative clothing lines for diverse children."
- **The "Why":** This is the heart of the matter—the underlying reason you're doing it at all. For me, it's because "I want children of color to see themselves reflected and celebrated in the world around them."

The "why" is where purpose resides. It's the driving force behind our choices and actions, the thing that gets us out of bed when motivation wanes. Without a "why," the "what" and "how" often lack meaning or staying power.

I'll be the first to admit that finding your "why" isn't always straightforward, but it begins with self-reflection. Here's a simple framework that has helped me and that can help you uncover your "why":

1. **What Are You Passionate About?** What topics, activities, or causes light a fire in your soul? Think about the moments when time seems to fly because you're so immersed in what you're doing.
2. **What Problems Do You Want to Solve?** Consider the issues or challenges that tug at your heart. What injustices bother you? What gaps do you see in the world that you feel called to fill?
3. **What Impact Do You Want to Make?** Imagine a future where your work or actions have made a

difference. What does that look like? Who benefits from what you do?
4. **What Values Are Most Important to You?** Reflect on the principles that guide your life—things like fairness, creativity, courage, or integrity. These values often reveal the foundation of your "why."

Now, take a moment to look at your answers. Do you see any common threads or themes? These recurring ideas are likely pointing you toward your core "why." Try to articulate this "why" in a single sentence. For example, "My 'why' is to empower others to..." or "My 'why' is to create a world where..." This will be your "why" statement. It will serve as your compass, guiding you even when the path gets tough.

My "Why" Statement

_____

_____

_____

Your "why" doesn't have to be grand or world-changing. It doesn't have to involve building an empire, solving global problems, or becoming famous. Purpose can be deeply personal. It could be raising a loving family, supporting your community, or pursuing a creative outlet that brings you joy.

The key is that your "why" resonates with you. It's about what matters to you, not what society or others say should matter. Purpose is as unique as a fingerprint, shaped by your experiences, values, and dreams.

With your statement in hand, consider how you can start living your "why" today. What small steps can you take to align your actions with your passions, address the problems you care about, and make the impact you desire? Even small steps taken consistently can lead to significant change over time.

Why Purpose Fuels Persistence

When you're grounded in purpose, you can face obstacles with a clarity that transcends fear and doubt. Purpose becomes your anchor in the storm, reminding you why you started and why it's worth continuing. This clarity doesn't eliminate challenges, but it does give you the resilience to overcome them.

For me, my "why" was rooted in representation. The vision of my daughter seeing herself in the world around her kept me going when doors closed and challenges loomed. Purpose reminded me that this wasn't just about creating a product; it was about creating a movement—one that celebrated children who had too often been overlooked.

Purpose transforms audacity into action and persistence into progress. It gives us the courage to take the leap and the tenacity to keep climbing, even when the path is steep. It's the foundation of every meaningful endeavor, and it's the spark that turns dreams into reality.

Purpose and Perseverance in Action

When individuals are deeply connected to their "why," they can navigate even the toughest challenges with determination and audacity. These real-life examples showcase the power of purpose to drive action, overcome obstacles, and create meaningful change.

Audacious

Social Activism: Malala Yousafzai
Malala Yousafzai's fight for girls' education is a testament to the power of purpose-driven audacity. Growing up in Pakistan's Swat Valley under the Taliban's rule, Malala's "why" was crystal clear: She believed that every girl deserved the right to learn. Despite death threats, she continued to speak out publicly about the importance of education. At just fifteen years old, she was shot by a Taliban gunman, a brutal attempt to silence her voice. Yet Malala refused to let fear define her journey. Her unwavering commitment to her purpose fueled her recovery and led her to become the youngest Nobel Peace Prize laureate. Today, she continues her mission through the Malala Fund, advocating for millions of girls worldwide. Her story shows that even in the face of life-threatening obstacles, staying true to one's purpose can inspire change on a global scale.

Sports: Serena Williams
Serena Williams's dominance in tennis is not just a story of talent but one of unrelenting purpose and perseverance. As a Black woman in a predominantly white and male-dominated sport, Serena faced racism, sexism, and criticism throughout her career. Her "why" went beyond winning championships—it was about breaking barriers, inspiring future generations, and showing that greatness knows no boundaries. Despite injuries, personal setbacks, and criticism about her body and character, Serena's determination to redefine the sport and create opportunities for others kept her moving forward. Her story exemplifies how a purpose rooted in representation and empowerment can drive someone to reach extraordinary heights.

Entrepreneur: Rihanna
As the founder of Fenty Beauty, Rihanna's journey into entrepreneurship was fueled by a clear purpose—to create a beauty brand that would be truly inclusive. Noticing the lack of makeup options for people with diverse skin tones, she launched Fenty Beauty in 2017 with forty foundation shades (now expanded to fifty). Her brand disrupted the beauty industry, making inclusivity a central focus and empowering people worldwide to feel represented and celebrated.

Social Justice: Bryan Stevenson
Bryan Stevenson, a lawyer and founder of the Equal Justice Initiative (EJI), has dedicated his life to fighting for justice for those wrongly imprisoned, unfairly sentenced, or forgotten by the legal system. His "why" is deeply personal: He believes that everyone deserves dignity and equality, regardless of their circumstances. Despite facing opposition, systemic racism, and limited resources, Bryan has successfully exonerated over 135 wrongly convicted death row prisoners and brought national attention to issues of mass incarceration. His unwavering commitment to his purpose has not only changed individual lives but also sparked broader conversations about equity and reform.

These stories show that when individuals are deeply connected to their purpose, they can achieve extraordinary feats. Whether it's fighting for education, overcoming physical challenges, nurturing vulnerable children, breaking barriers in sports, or advocating for justice, their "why" becomes the fuel that propels them forward, even in the face of immense obstacles.

Powering Past Obstacles to Fulfill Your Purpose: A Practical Exercise

Just because you're clear on your "why" doesn't mean the path will be linear and easy. Pursuing your purpose is rarely a smooth journey. Challenges and obstacles will inevitably arise, testing your commitment and resolve. The key to staying on course is recognizing these obstacles, understanding their impact, and taking deliberate, audacious actions to overcome them. This exercise will help you identify the hurdles that might occur on your path and develop strategies to move forward.

Step 1: Reflect on Your Purpose
Before addressing obstacles, you must be clear on who you're here to serve and your purpose for doing so. Answer the following prompts:

- What is my "why"? (Think about your core motivation—the deep reason behind your actions.)
- Who or what will benefit if I fulfill this purpose? (E.g., your family, your community, yourself.)
- How does pursuing this purpose align with my values and passions?

Write your answers down and keep them visible. This is the foundation you'll return to when obstacles arise.

Step 2: Identify Potential Obstacles
Now, consider the challenges you might face while pursuing your purpose. Be honest and thorough. You might not know

everything you will encounter up front, but this is an exercise you can refer back to again and again when you do encounter an unforeseen obstacle while on your journey. Use these prompts:

- What fears or doubts hold me back? (E.g., fear of failure, imposter syndrome, lack of confidence.)
- What external barriers might arise? (E.g., financial struggles, lack of resources, unsupportive environment.)
- What internal barriers might I face? (E.g., procrastination, lack of discipline, mental or emotional roadblocks.)
- What setbacks have I faced in the past, and how did I respond to them?

Write a list of potential obstacles, grouping them into internal (self-driven) and external (circumstantial) challenges.

Step 3: Use Your "Why" as Motivation and Fuel
For each obstacle you've identified, reflect on how your "why" can help you push past it. Ask yourself:

- How does this challenge test my commitment to my purpose?
- What will happen if I let this obstacle stop me?
- How will overcoming this obstacle bring me closer to fulfilling my purpose?

Step 4: Turn Your "Why" into an Encouraging Affirmation
Write a brief affirmation for each obstacle that reminds you of your "why." Declare this affirmation when the going gets hard to keep yourself encouraged. For example:

- **Obstacle:** Fear of failure
  Affirmation: "Every failure is a lesson that brings me closer to the impact I want to create."
- **Obstacle:** Financial challenges
  Affirmation: "My purpose is worth the investment, and I will find creative solutions to fund my dream."

Step 5: Create an Action Plan
Now it's time to take audacious actions. For each obstacle, brainstorm at least one actionable step you can take to overcome it. Use the following structure:

- **Obstacle:** Name the challenge.
- **Audacious Action:** Define one bold, specific step to address it.
- **Support System:** Identify who or what can help (e.g., a mentor, a resource, or a mindset shift).

Here's an example:

- **Obstacle:** Lack of resources to fund my purpose.
- **Audacious Action:** Research and apply for three funding opportunities (e.g., grants, partnerships, crowdfunding).

- **Support System:** Reach out to a mentor or someone in my network who has successfully funded a similar project.

Write out your full action plan and prioritize which steps you'll tackle first.

Step 6: Commit to Reassess and Reconnect Regularly
Obstacles are rarely one-time events; they often resurface in different forms. Schedule regular check-ins with yourself to reassess your challenges and progress. Use these prompts during your check-ins:

- Have I encountered new obstacles? If so, what are they?
- How have I successfully overcome challenges since my last check-in?
- Am I still connected to my "why"? If not, what do I need to do to reignite that connection?

This process ensures that you stay grounded in your purpose while maintaining the flexibility to adapt to new challenges.

Step 7: Celebrate Small Victories
Pursuing your purpose is a journey, not a race. Acknowledge the progress you've made, no matter how small. Each step forward, each obstacle overcome, is a testament to your commitment and resilience. Write down your victories as reminders of your strength and determination.

If you use this exercise, you will be empowered to recognize obstacles, reconnect with your purpose, and take audacious action to overcome challenges. Purpose-driven perseverance requires consistent effort, but with clarity, planning, and determination, you can power past any obstacle and fulfill your "why."

The Power of Audacious Purpose

Living a life of audacious purpose isn't just about having a "why"—it's about becoming unstoppable. This is your moment. When you choose to live for something bigger than yourself, you unlock a power that no obstacle, rejection, or failure can take away from you. That power is you—fueled by your vision, strengthened by your resilience, and ready to rise no matter what comes your way.

Your purpose isn't just a personal quest; it's a force for transformation. When you lean fully into it, you don't just change your life—you change the lives of the people around you. You become the kind of person who inspires others to dream bigger, try harder, and believe more deeply in what's possible. Your courage creates ripples that reach far beyond what you can see today.

Remember this: **Every challenge you face is a test of how badly you want the life you've envisioned.** And every time you keep going—every time you refuse to quit—you prove to yourself just how powerful you are. This is how mountains are moved, how legacies are built, how the impossible becomes reality.

You are ready. You have everything you need to crush the obstacles ahead. The world is waiting for the impact only you can make. Go out there and give it everything you've got. Live your purpose boldly, unapologetically, and audaciously. You've got this.

CHAPTER 8

Ignite Your Connections

LET ME TELL YOU about the day I dared to dream of partnering with Michelle Obama. It wasn't a moment of perfect confidence or a flawless plan—it was a moment of audacity. Could I, someone running a children's brand, really connect with one of the most influential women in the world? It felt impossible. But activating your network isn't about playing small or waiting for the perfect moment. It's about stepping into your purpose boldly, believing in your mission, and trusting that the right connections will come when you need them most.

The vision began as a spark: a project that could create real change. Election season was approaching, and I wanted to use my brand to empower families and amplify the importance of voting. My idea? A "mommy and me" collection called *Her Future* under my children's brand, Elle Olivia. The collection would feature our character, Elle Olivia, and deliver a simple but powerful message: for kids, the sweatshirt would say *My Future Matters*; for moms, it would say *Her Future*.

It was a vision that felt deeply personal and impactful. But I knew that for this project to reach its full potential, I needed partners who shared my passion for purpose. That's when I thought of Michelle Obama. Her work with *voters* exemplified everything this collection stood for: empowerment, action, and shaping the future. The gap between my world and hers felt immense. How could I possibly reach her?

The answer wasn't in trying to make a cold call or hoping for a chance encounter. It hinged on activating my network. And the first step was making the ask.

With a blend of excitement and trepidation, I sent a message to my community. "I'm working on a project that could truly make an impact. Does anyone have connections or advice for reaching Michelle Obama or her team? Any guidance would mean the world." It wasn't a polished elevator pitch—it was an honest, heartfelt plea for support. And then, I waited.

The responses were immediate and inspiring. Friends encouraged me, former colleagues advised me, and others admired my gutsy ask. But one message stood out: "I do have a contact of someone on her team who reports to her and leads her bipartisan group. Let me make the introduction."

That introduction was unreal. I had long admired Michelle Obama, and then to be connected to her organization, When We All Vote, known for empowering communities to vote and engage in democracy, was incredible. It aligned perfectly with my project's mission. What started as a simple ask grew into a connection that opened doors I hadn't even imagined.

I was introduced to the When We All Vote team all by asking my network to connect me. The conversations that followed were full of energy and alignment. We shared a passion for purpose and brainstormed ways to collaborate. They loved the idea of the *Her Future* collection and saw how it could resonate with families, especially mothers, as they prepared to make their voices heard in the upcoming election.

The partnership with When We All Vote brought the *Her Future* collection to life in a way I couldn't have done alone. Together, we crafted a campaign that highlighted the importance of voting, not just as an individual act, but as a generational legacy.

The collection became more than just sweatshirts—it became a call to action. The messaging, *My Future Matters* for kids and *Her Future* for moms, symbolized the responsibility and hope that voting brings. It resonated deeply with families, sparking conversations about why every vote counts and how each person's choices shape the future.

When We All Vote helped amplify the campaign through their platform, ensuring the message reached a national audience. The partnership brought resources, visibility, and credibility to the project, allowing it to have an impact far beyond what I had initially imagined. What began as an idea for my children's brand became a movement that united mothers and children around the shared goal of creating a better future.

When I made the ask, I wasn't just seeking a contact; I was activating my network's collective wisdom and resources. The relationships I had cultivated over the years became a bridge, connecting me to something bigger than myself.

The collaboration with When We All Vote turned my bold dream into a tangible project. Together, we created something meaningful that reached far beyond what I could have achieved alone. It was a reminder that when you trust your network, you can accomplish audacious goals—even if the path looks different from what you first envisioned.

> **Audacious goals are rarely achieved in isolation because life is not a solo endeavor.**

While the project itself was cool and unique, I am sharing this story because there is power in activating who you know today. You must be audacious enough to step into your vision and let others help you on the journey.

Why Your Network Matters for Audacious Goals

Audacious goals are rarely achieved in isolation because life is not a solo endeavor. While it's easy to think of ambitious dreams as an individual journey, every success is tied to someone who supported, inspired, or challenged you along the way. Likewise, every failure is softened by those who remind you that you're not defined by your mistakes. Your network is the bridge between where you are and where you want to go, providing the resources, guidance, opportunities, and support that often lie beyond your immediate reach.

Your network includes:

- **Friends and Family:** The people who support you emotionally and often know your strengths better than you do.
- **Colleagues and Mentors:** Those who can provide guidance, resources, or introductions.
- **Acquaintances:** People you may not know well but who may be closer to the connections you need than you think.

Ignite Your Connections

A strong network offers more than just connections; it provides resources, support, and opportunities that can propel you forward. Research underscores the significant role of professional networking in career advancement. Notably, 85 percent of job positions are filled through personal or professional connections. By building and activating a strong network, you create an ecosystem of support that helps you push past obstacles, maximize your potential, and achieve goals that once seemed out of reach. The bigger your dream, the more essential it is to rely on the power of your network. Here are some of the other benefits of having a strong network:

1. **Access to Resources:** Your network can connect you to tools, funding, or materials that you may not have access to on your own.
2. **Opportunities:** People in your network can introduce you to opportunities you didn't know existed, opening doors to collaborations, partnerships, or career advancements.
3. **Guidance and Expertise:** Mentors or knowledgeable connections can offer valuable advice, insights, and expertise to help you navigate challenges.
4. **Emotional Support:** A strong network provides encouragement during tough times and celebrates with you in moments of success.
5. **Accountability:** Trusted people in your circle can help keep you focused, motivated, and aligned with your goals.

By activating and nurturing your network, you create a powerful ecosystem of support that not only helps you overcome obstacles but propels you toward your greatest aspirations.

> **The bigger your dream, the more essential it is to rely on the power of your network.**

Before we dive into the type of relationships you need in your network and how to cultivate them, I want to share with you some relational truths about the power of life-changing relationships.

Relational Truths: The Power of Life-Changing Relationships

Truth #1: Life-changing relationships are few and far between, so honor them when you find them. The strongest relationships aren't about quantity, but quality. We might cross paths with countless individuals, but only a select few are destined to step in and become the allies, mentors, or champions we never knew we needed. These relationships bring unique skills, insights, and networks that align perfectly with our journey and become a crucial link in the chain of our story. Honor them by nurturing and investing in them over time.

Truth #2: Each life-changing relationship leaves an indelible mark on your life, often in ways you don't realize until later. Some arrive as mentors, others as friends. These individuals don't just cross your path—they illuminate it, forcing you to see things about yourself and the world that would otherwise remain in shadow.

Truth #3: Life-changing relationships require an open heart and a discerning mind. Not everyone who crosses your path is meant to stay, and not everyone who stays is meant to teach. But when you recognize that someone is uniquely placed in your life, it becomes your responsibility to lean into that connection, no matter how uncomfortable it might be at times.

There's humility required in receiving the lessons these people bring. Sometimes they come wrapped in love and encouragement, and other times they come wrapped in conflict or challenge. Both are gifts. When you resist the urge to write off a difficult interaction or a challenging person, you create space for transformation. Learning to receive also means letting go of preconceived ideas about who your "helpers" should be.

Truth #4: Life-changing relationships carry a specific lesson for you. From one, you may learn the power of resilience. They may model what it looks like to keep going when life is unrelenting, teaching you to dig deeper within yourself. From another, you might learn the beauty of vulnerability, the way sharing your struggles can deepen relationships and create spaces of healing.

Some teach you about boundaries—when to say no, when to step away, and when to protect your peace. Others teach you about abundance, showing you the value of generosity and collaboration. Perhaps most importantly, life-changing relationships teach you about yourself. They highlight your capacity for love, your ability to grow, and your willingness to change.

And then there are those who teach through contrast—who show you what you don't want, who push you to make decisions that align more closely with your values. These lessons are just as valuable as the ones taught through harmony and shared vision.

Truth #5: Just as life-changing relationships change your life, you are also here to change someone else's life. Your story, your strengths, and even your struggles can become someone else's source of encouragement or clarity. For one you might offer your authenticity—the willingness to show up fully as yourself and to share your journey honestly. To another you might offer a listening ear, a word of encouragement, or a reminder of their worth. Or maybe you will challenge someone to grow, holding them accountable or modeling a different way of being. What you offer doesn't have to be grand or profound. Often, it's the small, consistent acts of kindness, truth, and presence that leave the deepest impact.

Ultimately, life-changing relationships are gifts, even when they don't always feel like it. They shape you, strengthen you, and remind you that you were never meant to walk this road alone.

Assigned Relationships Versus Cultivated Relationships

Now that we know the purpose of relationships, let's look at who should be in our network. There are two types of life-changing relationships that make up your network:

Intentionally cultivated relationships are those you actively seek to build and maintain. These relationships are built through intentionality, requiring time, focus, and a genuine commitment to connection. Often these connections come from

Ignite Your Connections

deliberate effort—joining communities, engaging with mentors, and nurturing mutual respect with those whose values and goals align with your own. Building this type of network requires intentionality: Be genuine in your interactions, offer value without expecting immediate returns, and diversify your relationships to include a broad range of perspectives.

Assigned relationships, on the other hand, are the ones that enter your life for a purpose, but it often seems like coincidence. Their presence is often unplanned but profoundly impactful and divinely orchestrated. They arrive not when it's convenient but when it's necessary for your growth and journey. They come along during a pivotal moment, and you may recognize their significance only in hindsight.

These relationships challenge you, comfort you, or remind you of your purpose when you need it most. Trying to control who these people will be or how they'll enter our lives is futile; their assignment isn't ours to dictate. Instead, it's about remaining open to the possibility that someone, somewhere, is positioned to help carry us forward in ways we couldn't have orchestrated on our own.

Assigned relationships are more than allies—they involve those rare individuals placed in your path when you cannot advocate for yourself. They step into rooms you can't reach, speak your name with conviction, and embody your vision and values with unshakable respect. They champion your potential, ensuring your presence and purpose extend beyond the spaces you physically occupy. They're the bridges to new opportunities, the validation of your capabilities, and the resonance of your intentions. These are not just people in your corner; they're the ambassadors of your work, carrying your name forward and amplifying your impact, even when you're not around to do it yourself. This assigned person spoke truth to my intentions and amplified my presence when I was not around to do so myself.

You don't get to choose who is assigned to you, who will see the spark in your vision and decide to carry it forward with you. It's a mysterious alignment of timing, purpose, and often, something far beyond our understanding. We can prepare, position ourselves, and make ourselves ready for opportunity, but the people who come into our lives as true advocates arrive on their own terms, with their own reasons, and often in ways we couldn't anticipate. They are guided by something larger than our plans, drawn to support us not by force or request, but by a sense of connection that is deeply rooted and often instant.

Together, these two types of connections—those assigned to you and those you intentionally create—form a network that supports, inspires, and propels you toward your audacious goals.

Let me share with you two stories that highlight each of these types of relationships—cultivated and assigned—and the power of activating your network. In the first story, you will see how I intentionally cultivated a relationship that opened the door for me to a life-changing sponsorship, and in the second story you will see how an assigned person advocated for me in a room I wasn't even in, paving the way for an incredible opportunity. Both types of relationships are pivotal for an audacious life.

Special: The Power of Intentionally Cultivating Your Network

In 2019, I was relentlessly focused on building Boss Women Media, "a media company that is focused on creating community, tools, and resources for women to create the career of their dreams." I was pouring my heart, soul, and every dollar I had into creating spaces where women could connect, celebrate one another, and share their stories of triumph. It was so fulfilling curating these moments and crafting experiences that brought inspiration and community into beautiful settings. At the time, most of my funding came from my own pocket, with only a handful of sponsorships secured each year, barely reaching $25,000. While these sponsorships were instrumental in the bottom line and produced enough revenue so I could stay in business, I held on to one unwavering belief: Bigger sponsors would come, and they would come through people placed by God—strategically placed in my path, uniquely aligned with my mission, ready to help shape not only my future but theirs as well. I just didn't know how or when these people would show up.

As I was building Boss Women Media, I was often invited to speak at various events—mostly in women-centered spaces. On one occasion I was asked to lead a vision board workshop for a group of young girls. It was a packed day, with long stretches in the greenroom between sessions. And let me tell you, the greenroom was where it was at—stocked with the best snacks, thoughtful speaker gifts, and, most importantly, connections to sponsors. This event was backed by a financial institution, and I was determined to learn more about the people behind the scenes there.

One woman, in particular, caught my attention—an absolute force of positivity and purpose. Her name was Special, and she was just that. She worked for the financial company hosting the event, and she exuded a warmth and drive that felt almost otherworldly, like she was placed there just to lift others up. Casually, I shared with her what I was building, my passion for bringing women together, and I mentioned an upcoming event. Then, I intentionally went for it—I asked if her company ever sponsored events like mine. In networking, it's fairly commonplace to share about your business and vision with others, but it was audacious of me to ask about sponsorships. To my surprise, she responded with an enthusiastic "yes," handed me her contact information, and we parted ways. I didn't overthink it, but I felt my audacious intentionality had landed a connection that I knew would lead to something. I sent her a quick email sharing more of Boss Women Media's capabilities, that it was great to meet her, and how we should stay connected, along with my contact information.

A week later, an email from Special popped into my inbox, inviting me to present my organization's vision to her team. I was over the moon, and the timing couldn't have been better. I was ready to share an idea that I had been working on for months, and this financial institution would be the perfect partner to deliver the idea to. I poured two weeks into preparing a pitch that was customized to this brand—decked it out with creative visuals, powerful data, and a compelling story. This was my first six-figure pitch, a shot at securing a sponsor for a ten-city tour: *The Black Girl Magic Tour*, a summit designed to connect, empower, and equip Black women leaders and business owners with the resources they needed to succeed.

The night before the pitch, I meticulously planned every detail. I chose a crisp, white button-down and a sharp black-and-white plaid suit, styled my hair in its natural curls, and put on my signature red-orange lipstick. As I drove to the office, I whispered a prayer: "God, let the right voice see and hear me, to amplify this work for Your glory."

Walking into the office, I recorded a brief message: "This is it! I'm pitching my first six-figure deal for a ten-city tour." Special met me at the entrance, her warm smile putting me at ease as she asked, "Are you ready?" Oh, I was ready.

After a presentation in front of twelve decision-makers from Dallas, DC, and New York City, and several follow-up meetings, I got a partnership deal. That one "yes" changed the trajectory of my entire business, and it wouldn't have happened without me intentionally cultivating a relationship with Special.

Cultivated relationships are built through intentionality, requiring time, focus, and a genuine commitment to connection. By prioritizing authenticity and mutual respect, these relationships become the foundation for meaningful collaboration and support, offering depth and value far beyond superficial interactions. While cultivated relationships grow through deliberate effort, it's equally important to remain open to moments that feel serendipitous—those unexpected connections that align perfectly with your journey. This is where my dear friend Sabrina comes in.

Sabrina: The Magic of Assigned Relationships

During the COVID-19 pandemic, while the world was shutting down, connections across the globe opened up like never before. With the help of Zoom, reaching out to people and expanding my network became easier and more efficient. This shift was my opportunity to build relationships that would help shape the future of my business. One such connection was Sabrina, introduced to me by someone in my network who knew she worked for an organization I needed to collaborate with. Initially, our relationship began as a transactional business partnership, but it quickly deepened into something more meaningful. Sabrina understood my vision and leaned in—not just as a colleague, but as someone truly invested in my goals.

At first, Sabrina worked for a company I hired to provide a service. Midway through our collaboration, she left that organization but didn't leave me behind. I'll never forget the email she sent: "When I get settled in my new position, I'm going to introduce you to the right people." True to her word, she followed through. Her introduction led to my company being connected with the largest organization in the world. That one act of advocacy didn't just end there—it sparked a chain reaction, connecting me to even more people and allowing my network to expand in ways I hadn't imagined.

Then, just as these doors were opening, life threw me a curveball. Three days after my daughter was admitted to the NICU, I was given the opportunity of a lifetime: to pitch my business to that very same organization. It was a moment of extraordinary tension—balancing the fear and exhaustion of watching my newborn fight for her health with the weight of preparing for what could be a transformative opportunity for my business.

I wasn't sure I could do it. My husband encouraged me, saying, "It might be a good distraction." Despite my hesitation, I decided to show up, not just for myself but for the dream I had been building.

The pitch felt surreal. Postpartum emotions and the stress of the NICU weighed heavily on me, but somehow, I delivered. The decision-makers were intrigued and excited, but the outcome was uncertain. They promised to finalize their decision in a couple of months, and I waited anxiously.

Then, on an ordinary day, I received the call. They had chosen me. And why? Because during a meeting, someone spoke up on my behalf. Sabrina—someone I didn't know—had championed me. She said, "I know her. She goes to my church, and I've heard her speak. If we don't go with her, we're foolish."

That moment was a revelation. Sabrina was an assigned relationship that I wasn't even aware of—someone who entered my life for a purpose I couldn't have foreseen. Her words, spoken in a room I wasn't even in, changed the trajectory of my business.

Sabrina wasn't the first divinely assigned person on my journey, nor will she be the last. These relationships are proof that activating your network is about more than networking; it's about investing in people and trusting that the seeds you plant today will grow in ways you may never see.

As both of my stories illustrate, relationships in your network—whether cultivated or divinely assigned—are essential to achieving audacious goals, and you need both. They are the lifelines that carry us through challenges, open doors, and remind us that we're never alone on the journey. Every person you meet has the power to transform not just your business, but your life.

While I love assigned relationships, we do not have control over their entrance into our lives, and they are unique to our own story. So I want to focus on cultivated relationships. This will provide you with practical ways you can intentionally grow because this is what is within our control.

Strategies for Building a Strong Network

You may be wondering how to go about building your network. I am glad you asked. I'm going to share with you secrets to growing your network that have taken me more than a decade to learn. But you're going to be able to put them into action right away and see amazing results in both your personal and professional life. These steps are a mix of both strategic actions and an inner mindset shift. When you put these into action, you'll build an incredible network ready to help you fulfill your audacious dreams.

1. **Shift Your Mindset About Networking**

    The best place to start is by realizing that a network is more than a list of names. It's a dynamic web of relationships, each with its own potential to unlock opportunities. Activating your network is not just about tapping your contacts—it's about recognizing the power of the relationships you've nurtured, including friends, family, colleagues, and acquaintances, and aligning your vision with their potential to support you. When you have this mentality and share your vision authentically and invite others to contribute, you create a magnet for collaboration.

2. **Start with Existing Relationships**

    Begin by identifying friends, family, colleagues, mentors, and acquaintances who might offer valuable insights or opportunities. Reconnect with those you've lost touch with by sending a thoughtful message or scheduling a casual coffee chat. Share your goals openly and take the time to listen to their perspectives—you may uncover unexpected opportunities through these conversations.

3. **Expand Your Circle with Intention**

    Expanding your network requires intentional action and a willingness to step outside your comfort zone. Look for ways to meet people beyond your immediate circle by joining professional associations, local clubs, or online communities aligned with your interests or industry. Attend conferences, workshops, and meetups where you can connect with like-minded individuals. Leverage platforms like LinkedIn to find professionals whose work inspires you—follow their content, engage with their posts, and send personalized connection requests that explain why you'd like to connect. By building on existing relationships and seeking new connections strategically, you can create a robust, diverse network that opens doors and supports your goals.

4. **Build Genuine Relationships**

    Focus on building meaningful connections by prioritizing an understanding of others' goals, challenges, and passions. Approach networking as an opportunity to learn and support rather than to seek favors. Offer your time, expertise, or resources generously, knowing that true relationships are built on mutual value and trust. Introductions are often facilitated by genuine relationships you have nurtured and cultivated.

5. **Intentionally Keep in Touch**

    Reach out to people in your network regularly—not just when you need something. Ask how you can support them, and share updates about your journey without an agenda. This keeps you top-of-mind for opportunities. I often send a quick email or message like this to someone in my network: "Hi! I wanted to share a recent milestone in my business and see how things are going for you. Let me know if there's a way I can be helpful!"

6. **Seek Mentors and Role Models**

    Identify individuals who have achieved what you aspire to and reach out with thoughtful messages explaining your admiration. Be specific about your ask, such as requesting advice on a challenge or feedback on a project. By learning from those who have walked the path before you, you can gain insights and guidance that propel you forward.

7. **Diversify Your Network**

    Expand your network to include people from different industries, cultures, and areas of expertise. Engaging with individuals outside your immediate field broadens your horizons, sparks creativity, and introduces you to opportunities you might never have considered.

Ignite Your Connections

8. **Stay Open and Trust the Process**

   Sometimes key relationships don't come in the package you expect. They might not be in your industry or seem like the obvious choice to help you. Stay open to connections that feel serendipitous or unconventional. Say yes to opportunities to meet new people, even if they don't seem directly relevant. Trust that every interaction has the potential to lead to something greater.

By following these principles, you'll cultivate a network that's not only expansive but also deeply supportive, offering the connections, insights, and opportunities needed to achieve your goals.

Activating Your Network: Making the Audacious Ask

Now that you've found and intentionally connected with your people—those who align with your vision—let's talk about how we can actually activate these connections to help you fulfill your vision by making an audacious ask. Here are the "why," "what," "how," and "when" steps I work through when making an ask of my network.

Why to Ask for Help—Be Collaborative and Connected

It doesn't matter whether you're a mom pitching a new idea to your local PTA or a corporate executive pitching a new strategy for a company, sooner or later you are going to have something you want to rally people around, just like when I asked my network to help me get connected with Michelle Obama. When you bring others into your vision, you not only increase your chances of success, but you also create something bigger and more impactful than you could have achieved alone. Shared goals lead to shared victories. Here's how you can do this in a practical way.

- **Action Step:** Think of one person in your network who can help move your idea forward. Reach out to them and clearly share what you're working on and one specific way they can support you.
- **Example:** Write them a simple email. For example: "Hey, [Name], hope you're doing great! I wanted to share something I'm super excited about. I'm building [mention project]. Since you're so great at [mention their strength], I was wondering if you might be able to [specific ask]. Thanks in advance for your time and consideration."

What to Ask for Help with—Be Strategic and Vision-Focused
Ask for help with fulfilling your audacious vision—whether that be through resources, advice, feedback, or an open door. People are drawn to clear vision. When you know what you're building, why it matters, where you're headed, and which audience needs your vision or would make great partners, it becomes easier for others to recognize how they can support you.

- **Action Step:** Write down your vision and the goals you're working toward. Be specific. Share this vision with trusted individuals in your network so they can advocate for you when opportunities arise.
- **Example:** Instead of "I run a business," say, "I'm building a children's lifestyle brand that helps

Ignite Your Connections

families of color celebrate big possibilities through affirmations and representation."

How to Ask for Help—Be Clear and Specific
When reaching out to your network, be clear and specific about what you're asking for—whether it's advice, an introduction, or feedback. When you articulate what you need, it gives others the opportunity to connect you with the right person or resource.

- **Action Step:** Write down your ask as clearly and specifically as possible.
- **Example:** Instead of "I'm looking for help with marketing," try "I'm looking for someone with experience in digital campaigns who can give me feedback on my strategy. Do you know anyone I should talk to?"

When to Ask for Help—Be Proactive
The best time to ask for help is before you feel overwhelmed or stuck. Waiting until the last minute often limits your options and creates unnecessary stress. Instead, view asking for help as part of your strategy from the start. When you're clear on what you need and who can help, you position yourself to move forward with confidence and efficiency.

- **Action Step:** As soon as you identify a challenge or gap in your plan, take ten minutes to write down what you need help with and who might be able to support you. Then, reach out early to avoid last-minute pressure.

- **Example:** When I was preparing for my big pitch, I asked a friend skilled in storytelling if they could provide feedback to help me refine my presentation and build a stronger narrative.

The Power of Reciprocity: Giving Back to Your Network

We've talked a lot about how your network can help you once activated. Now let's talk about how you can give back to your network. Here's the truth... networking is a two-way street; the strength of your network depends on what you contribute to it as much as what you gain from it. True reciprocity is about offering value, support, and opportunities to the people in your circle, creating a cycle of mutual growth and trust.

People are often drawn to those who are willing to give as much as they receive. When you help others, you create a ripple effect of generosity that often circles back to you. Look for opportunities to share your expertise, make introductions, or lend support to others in your network. Be intentional about adding value to others' lives or businesses. For example, if you know someone struggling with a challenge you've faced, offer advice or resources: "I remember going through something similar. Here's what worked for me—hope it's helpful!" Here are some other quick ways you can offer value to others:

- Make an introduction that aligns with someone's goals.
- Share valuable resources or insights to help someone succeed.
- Show up to offer encouragement or advice during challenging times.

Ignite Your Connections

- Connect a colleague with a mentor who can guide them.
- Recommend someone for an opportunity that suits their skills.
- Celebrate someone's achievements by amplifying their work to your own network.

When you give generously, you build relationships rooted in trust and collaboration, ensuring that your network thrives as a true partnership. For example, after a mentor helped me refine my pitch, I returned the favor by connecting them with someone in my network who could support their business expansion. It was a small act, but it reinforced that our relationship was a two-way street. Giving back doesn't have to be monumental—it's about showing up when it matters.

> **The strength of your network depends on what you contribute to it as much as what you gain from it.**

Unleash the Power of Your Network

Your network isn't just a tool—it's the launchpad to an audacious, limitless life. It's where dreams transform from ideas into action, and where the support, wisdom, and energy of others amplify your impact. This is your secret weapon, your edge. The truth is, you are one relationship away from the breakthrough you've been waiting for. One conversation, one connection, one moment of courage could catapult you into opportunities you never thought possible.

The people in your network are not just contacts—they're catalysts. They are the ones who will believe in your vision when self-doubt creeps in, champion your ideas in spaces you've never entered, and challenge you to dream bigger than you've dared before. But here's the kicker: The power of your network is not in simply knowing people. It's in *cultivating* those relationships with intention and authenticity. That's the key to creating partnerships that multiply your potential.

So here's my pep talk for you: You are standing on the brink of the most transformative season of your life. If you choose to invest in your relationships—with humility, generosity, and courage—you will find yourself supported in ways you never thought possible. Step boldly into this moment. Nurture the connections you already have. Seek out those who inspire you. Speak your dreams aloud and invite others into your journey.

> **You are one relationship away from the breakthrough you've been waiting for.**

Because when you build and nurture your network, you aren't just chasing success—you're creating a legacy. You're stepping into the kind of life that people write books about. And you are *more than ready* for it.

CHAPTER 9

Finding Your Voice: How to Craft an Audacious Pitch

PITCHING IS MY SUPERPOWER. Over the years, I've had the privilege of pitching deals with some of the largest brands in the world—Amazon, Disney, Target, Cash App, Capital One, Square, Intuit, Mailchimp, Salesforce, and countless others. But here's the truth: Pitching isn't magic, and it's not reserved for the fearless or the lucky. It's a skill anyone can learn. With unshakable confidence and clear, simple communication, you can turn your ideas into opportunities and your vision into reality. And I'm here to show you how. But let me be honest—the biggest mistake I've made in pitching over the years was making the pitch about *me*. The turning point came when I realized the power of shifting focus: making the pitch about the person on the other side of the table and the value

I could create for *them*. This one change transformed how I pitch—and it will transform how you do too.

Here's the thing: *Anyone* can use this formula. A college student seeking an internship. Someone gunning for a promotion. Or even someone dreaming of partnering with a Fortune 100 company. This framework is game-changing, and it's within your reach.

The real magic lies in your ability to clearly communicate your value. Confidently expressing who you are, what you offer, and what you stand for is a game-changer—not just in pitching, but in creating an audacious life. An audacious person doesn't shy away from opportunity; they put themselves out there and boldly articulate their worth.

You have the power to craft and deliver compelling messages that open doors to opportunities in every area of your life. Whether it's in your career, relationships, or personal goals, mastering this skill will set you apart and empower you to step fully into your potential. I'm not here to teach you perfection, because perfection is not required. I'm here to teach you how to deliver your pitch with audacity—grounded in authenticity and designed to connect and inspire action. If I can make this my superpower, so can you.

> **Value unspoken is value unrealized.**

Why Communicating Your Value Matters

Your value is your essence—the unique combination of your skills, experiences, and perspective that no one else can replicate. But here's the thing: Value unspoken is value unrealized.

Finding Your Voice: How to Craft an Audacious Pitch

No one can fully appreciate what you bring to the table if you don't have the courage and clarity to communicate it.

When you master the art of expressing your value, something profound happens.

1. **You Create Space for Opportunity**

    Opportunities don't just appear out of thin air—they're drawn to clarity and conviction. When you confidently communicate what you bring to the table, you make it easy for the right doors to open. It's not about luck or coincidence; it's about being intentional and unapologetic in showing up as your full self.

2. **You Inspire Others to Believe**

    Audacity isn't just about self-confidence; it's about creating belief. When you boldly express your value, you spark something in others. You inspire them to see potential where they might have overlooked it. You invite them to dream bigger, act boldly, and take a chance on you.

3. **You Challenge the Status Quo**

    To communicate your value is to challenge a world that too often wants you to stay quiet, to wait your turn, to fit neatly into someone else's expectations. It's a radical act of self-respect, a way of declaring, "I belong here, and I'm bringing everything I've got." Audacity is what transforms that declaration into action.

Mic-Drop Moments: Speak with Confidence and Clarity

Living audaciously means being unafraid to stand in your truth and proclaim your worth. When you solidify the mic-drop moments for yourself, you will always be able to speak your truth—whether it's about your value, your mission, or your vision—and it goes beyond just words. It demands you to show up and deliver realness, simplicity, boldness, and connectivity. Here are four game-changing principles to help you deliver your ideas and concepts in a way that leaves a lasting impact:

1. **Make It Real:** You can't speak your truth when you are trying to sound like someone else. So don't. Deliver it from your own uniqueness.

    Mic-Drop Moment Mastery: People can sense when you are real and when you are fake. Being authentic and real is magnetic. Speak from your heart, and your truth will land with undeniable force.

2. **Make It Simple:** Powerful messages are never long and complex. Instead, they are simple and sharp. Speak in a way that is clear, direct, and unforgettable.

    Mic-Drop Moment Mastery: Your ideas or concepts don't need to be overly decorated with fluff—precision is the secret here. Say less and mean more.

3. **Make It Bold, Not Perfect:** Waiting for the "perfect moment" or the "perfect words" will keep you silent forever. Boldness isn't about having it all figured out; it's about choosing to show up anyway.

Finding Your Voice: How to Craft an Audacious Pitch

Mic-Drop Moment Mastery: Confidence isn't the absence of fear—it's the presence of courage.

4. **Make It Connective:** You must connect with the audience before you convince them. Learn about them and what they value.
Mic-Drop Moment Mastery: Speak to your audience, not at them. Connection is the bridge that turns your truth into a transformational moment.

These principles aren't just about crafting words—they're about commanding presence, creating connection, and leaving no doubt about who you are and what you stand for. A mic-drop moment isn't an accident; it's the result of speaking your truth with audacity and clarity. And when you master this, you don't just speak—you shift the room.

Before diving into the art of pitching, it's important to take a step back and ask: Why does this matter? At first glance, pitching might seem like something reserved for entrepreneurs or salespeople—those whose work explicitly requires them to sell ideas, products, or services. But the truth is, we're all pitching, all the time. Whether you're presenting an idea in a meeting, advocating for yourself in a job interview, or simply trying to express your needs in a personal relationship, you're engaging in a form of pitching.

The common thread? Communication. Finding your voice and learning to communicate with clarity and confidence isn't just about speaking your truth—it's about connecting with others in a way that moves them to action. And that's exactly what a pitch does.

> **Living audaciously means being unafraid to stand in your truth and proclaim your worth.**

This is why I'm zeroing in on pitching. It's not just a tool for entrepreneurs; it's a framework for anyone looking to be heard, understood, and impactful. By mastering this skill, you're equipping yourself to navigate a world where your ability to articulate your ideas can open doors, create opportunities, and build meaningful connections—no matter your role or industry.

The Evolution of My Pitch

While I've long known how to pitch, I didn't always recognize where it began. My journey started much earlier than I realized—back when I was twelve years old, standing in front of a congregation, delivering church announcements. In those moments, I was learning how to **command attention, engage an audience, and communicate with clarity.** By my teenage years, I was leading children's church, breaking down messages in ways that inspired and connected with others.

What I didn't know then was that these experiences were shaping the foundation for everything that followed. They were teaching me **presence, confidence, and the power of my voice**—skills that would later serve me in interviews, in boardrooms, and eventually as a business owner.

Pitching has become more than just a skill for me—it's a **powerful tool** that has allowed me to thrive as a **public speaker, presenter, influencer, and motivator.** It has given me the ability to **articulate my vision with conviction, connect with people on a deeper level, and inspire action wherever**

Finding Your Voice: How to Craft an Audacious Pitch

I go. Whether I'm sharing my business ideas, advocating for myself, or encouraging others, my ability to pitch has been my greatest asset.

Where I once hesitated to bring my full self into corporate spaces, I now use my voice to **empower others to stand boldly in theirs**. Because true confidence isn't about fitting in—it's about **owning your presence, speaking your truth, and knowing that your voice has the power to change rooms, opportunities, and lives.**

When I started Boss Women Media, I had big dreams and plenty to say. I wanted to build something meaningful—something that would empower women, foster authentic connections, and provide the tools they needed to thrive. But here's what I realized: If I couldn't articulate what my business was about in a way that others could immediately understand, I couldn't expect them to believe in it. I had to evolve my pitch. I needed more than passion; I needed precision. The goal was to craft a single, powerful sentence that distilled everything—my mission, my audience, and my value—into something unforgettable. That process was humbling. Crafting a pitch seems simple on the surface, but it forces you to confront hard questions about who you are, who you serve, and what makes your vision unique. For me, it meant going back to the basics:

Who am I serving? Women—specifically ambitious women seeking community, inspiration, and resources to achieve their goals.

What problem am I solving? The lack of accessible, meaningful spaces for women to feel empowered, connected, and supported in their journeys.

What makes us unique? Boss Women Media isn't just a company—it's an experience. A place where women are inspired, informed, and welcomed into a community that values their growth.

I wrote draft after draft, talked it out with trusted friends and my husband, and kept refining. Each attempt brought me closer to the core truth, but the real breakthrough happened when I realized that my pitch couldn't just be a string of facts—it had to be a story. It needed to embody the heart of Boss Women Media: why we exist, not just what we do.

Finally, the pitch clicked:

> Boss Women Media is an offline and online women's empowerment community and media company, and we create experiences for women to connect and be resourced.

That single sentence wasn't just words—it was our story, captured in its purest form. It felt simple but substantial, clear yet powerful. It painted a picture of what we do and why it matters. It was more than a pitch; it became the foundation for how I communicated my vision to the world.

But the process didn't stop there. While the one-sentence pitch gave me clarity, it was the beginning of a broader story—one I could expand on when I needed to go deeper, connect emotionally, or inspire action.

Telling a Story with Your Pitch

Your pitch is a way to capture attention, inspire belief, and create connection in a single moment. Here is the framework you use to create your pitch before presenting it to your audience. I am going to walk you through step-by-step and give you an opportunity to craft your own message.

1. **Start with the Core Message:**
   - Who you are
   - What you do
   - Who is your target audience?

     For example: *Boss Women Media is an offline and online women's empowerment community and media company, and we create experiences for women to connect and be resourced.*

2. **Provide Context**

    A great story doesn't start and end with a sentence—it provides context. Briefly share the "why" behind your pitch. Explain the problem you saw or the need that inspired you. This creates an emotional connection and shows your audience the bigger picture.

    For example: *I saw a lack of spaces where ambitious women could feel empowered, connected, and supported, so I created a community where women could thrive.*

3. **Highlight the Unique Value**

    Your pitch should communicate what sets you apart, but your story should drive it home. Explain what makes your approach, perspective, or mission different—and why it matters.

For example: *We're not just a company; we're an experience. Boss Women Media is a space where women feel seen, supported, and inspired to take action.*

4. **Share Your Experience and Results**

   Use your pitch as a starting point, then build on it with specific examples or vivid imagery. Bring your mission to life with stories of the impact you've made or the people you've served.

   For example: *We've hosted events that bring hundreds of women together to network, learn, and grow, creating a ripple effect of empowerment in their careers and lives.*

5. **End with a Call to Action that Grabs the Audience's Attention**

   Every great story needs a memorable ending. Tie it back to your audience, leaving them with a clear takeaway or a call to action. Help them see how your story connects to them or how they can be part of it.

   For example: *If you're ready to connect with like-minded women and unlock the tools you need to succeed, Boss Women Media is for you.*

When you use your pitch as the anchor for your story, it becomes a clear, compelling narrative. It's not just a

Finding Your Voice: How to Craft an Audacious Pitch

statement—it's an invitation for others to believe in your vision and join you in your mission.

The refinement of my message from pitch to story opened doors to greater opportunities and collaborations. I found myself not only pitching to companies, but partnering with them, and not just speaking to audiences, but building lasting connections.

Now your turn! Write down your core message in one sentence that answers who, what, and how.

Here's the broader lesson: Whether it's for a business, a career opportunity, or a personal goal, refining how you communicate your value is a game-changer. It's not just about what you say—it's about how you make others feel and believe in your vision. Clarity is what unlocks opportunity, but audacity is what turns that opportunity into something extraordinary.

Your pitch, like your story, is ever-evolving. It grows with you, adapts to new challenges, and becomes sharper with each attempt. And when you can speak your value with confidence and clarity, you don't just tell people what you do—you invite them to believe in it with you. That's the real power of refining your message.

Here are some case studies that demonstrate ways you can pitch yourself in personal or professional settings.

Case Studies

Case Study 1: How to Pitch Yourself in a Job Interview
Scenario: Applying for a social media role at a sustainable goods company.
Pitch: "I know your team is looking for someone to drive engagement, especially around your sustainability efforts.

In my current role, I've led campaigns that boosted engagement by 40 percent, including one highlighting eco-friendly practices that went viral. I'm excited to bring my skills in creating impactful, engaging campaigns to help amplify your mission."

Takeaway: Connect your experience directly to their goals and show measurable impact.

Case Study 2: How to Pitch Yourself When Networking
Scenario: Meeting a senior executive at a networking event.
Pitch: "I've admired how your team has made AI tools accessible to small businesses. As a software engineer specializing in AI, I've developed tools that improved customer retention by 25 percent. I'd love to hear more about your approach and explore how I might contribute to your work in the future."
Takeaway: Be specific, highlight your expertise, and show interest in learning more.

Case Study 3: How to Pitch Your Needs to a Spouse
Scenario: Expressing your need for more shared responsibilities at home.
Pitch: "I've been feeling overwhelmed lately, and I realize I need more support from you. I know we both have a lot on our plates, but could we divide the household tasks differently? For example, if you could handle meal prep a few nights a week, it would give me more breathing room to recharge and focus on other things. I'd love to hear your thoughts on how we can make this work together."
Takeaway: Clearly express your feelings, specify your needs, and invite collaboration to find a solution.

Finding Your Voice: How to Craft an Audacious Pitch

Case Study 4: How to Pitch for a Raise/Promotion
Scenario: Asking for a promotion after two years of strong performance.
Pitch: "Over the past two years, I've consistently exceeded goals, including leading a project that boosted revenue by $500,000. I've also taken on leadership tasks, mentoring teammates and streamlining processes. I'd love to discuss a senior role where I can make an even greater impact."
Takeaway: Highlight key achievements and focus on your readiness for more responsibility.

Case Study 5: How to Pitch Your Professor for an Internship/Research Position
Scenario: Asking a professor to join their research team.
Pitch: "Dr. Lee, your research on regenerative medicine is fascinating. I've excelled in cell biology and gained lab experience with tissue culturing. I'd love to contribute as a research assistant and help support your work while learning from your expertise."
Takeaway: Be concise, show knowledge of their work, and explain how your skills align with their needs.

Those case studies help you see all the ways you can learn from the pitching method shared here.

The Art of Audacious Pitching

The Art of Audacious Pitching is a framework I use to land partnership deals from the top Fortune 100 companies around the world, and now you can do the same! Scan the QR code for step-by-step instructions to learn the method I use for The Art of Audacious Pitching.

Audacious

Unleashing the Power of Your Audacious Message

Communicating your ideas or concepts is more than a skill—it's a way to transform how you show up in every area of life. Whether you're pitching yourself for a dream job, advocating for your needs in a relationship, or presenting your next big idea, your voice is your most powerful tool. When used with clarity, confidence, and purpose, it can unlock opportunities, build connections, and help you create the life and career you've envisioned.

But here's the truth: This isn't about perfection. Crafting and delivering compelling messages takes practice. It requires refining your pitch, stepping outside your comfort zone, and learning from each attempt. The good news? The more you do it, the stronger and more audacious your voice becomes.

This is your blueprint for transformation. The way you shape and share your story holds the power to change everything. It's not just about pitching a product, idea, or vision—it's about owning your voice and stepping into the full weight of your potential. The stories you tell can open doors you didn't even know existed. They can ignite new relationships, amplify your confidence, and propel you toward goals that once felt out of reach.

Finding Your Voice: How to Craft an Audacious Pitch

But here's the truth: None of this happens by chance. It takes intention, courage, and a willingness to do the work. Start here. Start now. Build your pitch. Hone your story. Speak with the kind of boldness that leaves no doubt about your worth or your vision.

Every pitch is a chance to home in on your skills to tell a story. So don't hold back. Do the work. Lean into the discomfort. And when it's your time to speak, deliver with the kind of conviction that makes the world stop and listen.

This is your moment to create mic-drop stories that don't just move others—they move mountains.

Now go make it happen.

CHAPTER 10

"No" Starts the Convo

"NO" IS NEVER MY final answer—it's just the beginning of my next strategy. When I landed the deal to get my products on Target's shelves, it felt like a dream come true. But that dream came with a price tag: I needed over $400,000 to cover inventory costs. The odds were stacked against me, and rejection seemed to echo from every direction. But giving up was never on the table. I refused to let "no" define my outcome—instead, I let it fuel my determination to find a way forward.

I started by reaching out to a list of twenty friends and acquaintances—people I thought would believe in my vision enough to offer a bridge loan. Let me be clear: This wasn't a donation. It was a guarantee to be paid back with interest within thirty days of the products shipping to Target. But after countless phone calls and meetings, most of those people said no. And to be honest, I didn't even ask my family because I didn't have anyone in my family who could lend that kind of money.

Each rejection stung, but it didn't stop me. I moved on to the banks, walking into meeting after meeting with my pitch and my POs in hand, only to hear another *no*. Then I hit up two more banks—no. Next, I reached out to people I knew who might know people with money—no again. I even went to banks that specialize in financing against purchase orders, and two of them turned me down. Every avenue I pursued, every door I knocked on, came back with the same answer: *no*.

But here's what I learned: **A "no" is never the end of the story. A "no" is a fight. It's not a stop sign—it's a challenge.** Each rejection forced me to dig deeper, refine my approach, and push harder. And eventually, after hearing "no" so many times, I got the one "yes" that changed everything for me and taught me even more.

Rejection is a part of life, but how you respond to it determines the life you build. If you want to live audaciously—to achieve the kind of success most people only dream about—you have to reframe "no" as a stepping stone, not a stop sign. In the pages that follow, I'm going to show you how to harness the power of "no" to fuel your determination, refine your strategy, and unlock opportunities you never thought possible. These tools and mindsets can shift how you see rejection and, ultimately, how you see yourself. If you're ready to turn life's obstacles into the foundation for your boldest dreams, keep reading. This is where the magic begins.

> "No" is never my final answer—it's just the beginning of my next strategy.

The Power of "No"

A "no" isn't the end of your story—it's just a plot twist. Here's what I've come to understand about the word "no":

1. **A "No" Isn't About You**

   Rejection often has nothing to do with your worth, your abilities, or your vision. It's about timing, priorities, or resources. Understanding this helps you separate the "no" from your identity. It's not personal—it's logistical. That realization allows you to remove the emotion from the rejection and treat it like a puzzle to solve, rather than a verdict on your value.

2. **"No" Creates Clarity**

   Every "no" is valuable feedback. It tells you what's not resonating, what's missing, or where someone's concerns lie. That information is a gift. It allows you to sharpen your pitch, adapt your approach, and figure out exactly what it will take to get to a "yes." Without those rejections, I wouldn't have learned how to frame my ask better or target the right people.

3. **"No" Builds Resilience**

   Facing rejection strengthens you in ways success never can. Each time you hear "no" and keep going, you build the muscle of perseverance. You become more creative, more determined, and more equipped to navigate challenges. By the time I got to that one "yes," I had developed a level of grit I didn't even know I had.

So if you're facing rejection, remember: Every "no" is just a step on the way to your "yes." It's not about how many doors close in your face—it's about how many times you're willing to knock. When you fight against "no," you're not just fighting for your vision—you're building the strength, clarity, and resilience that will carry you to success. And trust me, that one "yes" makes every "no" worth it.

> To achieve the kind of success most people only dream about—you have to reframe "no" as a stepping stone, not a stop sign.

From "No" to "Yes"

The word "no" has a way of landing hard. It's sharp, final, and often feels like a judgment on your worth, ideas, or ability. But what if "no" isn't the end of the story? What if it's an invitation—a redirection that holds the power to transform not only your journey but also your perspective?

I've stood on the battlefield of rejection more times than I can count. I've heard "no" from friends, banks, investors, and decision-makers who didn't see the vision I was trying so hard to share. There were days when "no" felt insurmountable, like a door that would never open no matter how hard I knocked. But over time, I began to see "no" differently. It wasn't an end—it was a beginning.

Take, for instance, the funding story. Those rejections did not stop me. I knew eventually I would receive a "yes"; I just had to stay consistent. The "no" never stopped me, and I knew

"No" Starts the Convo

I had the power to reframe what I was experiencing. Instead of seeing rejection as failure, I saw it as redirection. I asked questions. I sought feedback. I dug into the reasons behind the "no" and learned how to refine my approach. Each rejection became a stepping stone—a moment of clarity that pushed me closer to the elusive "yes." And when that "yes" finally came, it wasn't just validation. It was proof that persistence, creativity, and resilience can break through even the hardest of walls. I want to share with you my strategy for how to fight back against "no" until you get a "yes."

How to Fight Back Against "No"

1. **Shift Your Mindset About Rejection**

   The first step in overcoming rejection is changing the way you see it. Instead of viewing "no" as a failure, see it as part of the process. Success isn't about avoiding rejection; it's about learning from it and moving forward. Reframe every "no" as an opportunity to grow, refine, and adapt.

2. **Ask the Right Questions**

   When someone says "no," don't just walk away. Use it as an opportunity to learn. Ask thoughtful questions like:
   - "Can you help me understand your concerns?"
   - "What would make this a better fit for you?"
   - "Is there a way we can revisit this conversation in the future?"

These questions show that you're open to feedback and willing to adapt, which can turn a "no" into a "maybe" or even a "yes" down the line.
3. **Prepare for Setbacks**
Rejection is inevitable, but how you prepare for it can make all the difference.
- *Know Your "Why"*: Stay anchored in your purpose. When rejection hits, reconnect with the reason you started in the first place.
- *Anticipate Objections*: Before pitching your idea, think through the reasons someone might say "no" and prepare responses to address their concerns.
- *Build a Support System*: Surround yourself with people who believe in your vision. Their encouragement will keep you going when the rejections start piling up.
4. **Pivot, Don't Quit**
Rejection isn't a signal to stop; it's an invitation to pivot. Use it as a chance to refine your approach, try a different angle, or explore new opportunities. Just because one door closes doesn't mean another won't open.

The Fight Against Burnout

Here's the part people don't often talk about: Hearing "no" over and over again can wear you down. It's exhausting to put your heart into something only to be met with resistance. I've lived on that street, and I know how quickly burnout can creep in when it feels like all you're doing is fighting against the tide.

But burnout doesn't mean you're weak, and it doesn't mean you're doing something wrong. In fact, it often happens to the most ambitious among us—the ones who refuse to settle, who believe in their vision so deeply they'll do anything to see it through. The secret to overcoming burnout isn't giving up; it's learning how to protect your energy and tend to the fire that drives you. Here are three strategies I use to keep myself from being burned out that can help you stay charged up too.

STRATEGY #1: Realize Rest Is Revolutionary
You can't fight for your dreams if you're running on empty. Rest isn't indulgent; it's necessary. When you honor your need to recharge, you show up sharper, stronger, and more prepared to face the next challenge.

STRATEGY #2: Say "No" to Say "Yes"
Every "yes" you give is a "no" to something else. Learning to discern where to invest your energy is a game-changer. Say "no" to distractions, guilt-driven commitments, and anything that doesn't align with your vision so you can say "yes" to what truly matters.

STRATEGY #3: Celebrate Progress
When you're constantly chasing the next goal, it's easy to overlook how far you've come. Take a moment to celebrate the small wins. Each step forward is a victory, and recognizing that keeps you fueled for the journey ahead.

When to Accept the "No"

Not every "no" is meant to be conquered. Sometimes, a "no" is a gift—a form of protection or redirection toward something better. The challenge is learning to discern when to keep pushing and when to step back, trust the process, and allow the bigger blessing to unfold.

Let me share a story about a time I had to accept a "no," even though everything in me wanted to fight against it.

When we were in the process of purchasing our second home, I had my heart set on a particular property. It wasn't just a house—it felt like a symbol of the life I wanted for my family. I envisioned us building memories there, hosting gatherings, and settling into a space that felt like ours. But when we went through the approval process, the numbers didn't align. Despite my determination, the bank wouldn't approve the loan.

At first, I was crushed. I couldn't understand why this was happening. I was used to finding a way, to pushing through obstacles, and to making things happen. But this time, the door was firmly closed. I was frustrated, questioning whether I'd done something wrong or hadn't fought hard enough.

Looking back, that "no" was one of the best things that ever happened to me.

Because I accepted the "no," we didn't stretch ourselves financially in ways that would have left us vulnerable. Instead, we waited and kept searching. Months later, the perfect home came onto the market—one that was not only better suited to our family's needs but also a better financial fit.

Sometimes, a "no" is a gift—a form of protection or redirection toward something better.

That home gave us the freedom and security we needed to thrive, and I realized that the earlier rejection wasn't a failure; it was protection.

How to Know When to Accept the "No"

It's not always easy to know whether a "no" is a sign to fight back or a signal to let go. Here are some foolproof ways to discern when a "no" is a signal to step back and let go:

Say "no" when:

- It compromises your values or well-being. If pursuing a "yes" requires you to sacrifice your integrity, your peace of mind, or your health, it's a sign to walk away.
- You're forcing something that doesn't align. Sometimes, you can feel yourself pushing harder than the situation warrants. If the path feels unnatural or overly strained, consider whether it's the right path for you.
- The timing isn't right. A "no" often means "not yet." Patience can reveal opportunities that are better aligned with your goals and circumstances.
- The cost outweighs the reward. If the pursuit of a goal is draining your resources—financial, emotional, or otherwise—it might be time to pause and reassess.

Accepting a "no" doesn't mean giving up. It means trusting that there's a bigger picture, one that you can't see in the moment. Letting go of what's not meant for you creates space for something better to come along. That's not just a mindset—it's a principle that can transform how you navigate rejection and disappointment.

> **Letting go of what's not meant for you creates space for something better to come along.**

The key is learning to differentiate between the "no" that challenges you to grow and the "no" that sets you up for the blessing you didn't even know you needed.

Turning "No" into Your Greatest Opportunity

The word "no" has the power to stop you in your tracks—or propel you toward your destiny. It's all about how you choose to respond. Now, we've explored the duality of "no": as both a challenge to overcome and a redirection toward something greater. This isn't just a lesson about rejection; it's a call to action for living an audacious, purpose-driven life.

Rejection is inevitable, but it's never final. It's an opportunity to refine your vision, deepen your resolve, and build resilience that will carry you through life's toughest moments. Each "no" is a reminder to pause, recalibrate, and press forward with boldness and clarity. Yet sometimes, a "no" is also a signal to step back, trust the process, and allow space for the blessing that's waiting just around the corner.

When you reframe rejection as redirection, you unlock its true power. That closed door might be protecting you from a path that isn't aligned with your purpose—or guiding you toward a greater opportunity you can't yet see.

So here's my challenge to you: The next time you face a "no," don't let it define you. Instead, let it refine you. Fight for the "yes" when it's right, but trust the "no" when it's necessary.

Use every rejection as fuel to grow stronger, wiser, and more determined.

And most importantly, remember this: **You are never defeated by a "no."** You're only redirected. The blessings that await you often require patience, perseverance, and trust in the journey. Don't give up. The "yes" you're fighting for—or the one waiting beyond the "no"—is closer than you think.

Keep showing up. Keep believing. Keep knocking on doors. Because the life you're building is worth every challenge, every redirection, and every audacious step forward.

CHAPTER 11

The ROI of Investing in Yourself

IMAGINE TRYING TO FUEL a fire with no spark or expecting a harvest from barren soil. It's impossible, right? Yet, so often, we pour our time, energy, and resources into everything and everyone around us while neglecting the most important investment of our lives—the one we make in ourselves. Here's the truth: If you want to live boldly, to transform your life, and to take audacious steps toward your dreams, you must prioritize *you*. Because the reality is, you cannot ignite greatness in the world if you're running on empty.

Personal investment is the cornerstone of transformation—it's the bold decision to believe in your potential and commit wholeheartedly to your growth. But you know what it requires: audacity. The courage to believe you're worthy of investing in. Building an extraordinary life requires a reservoir of strength rooted in physical, mental, and emotional well-being. When you invest in yourself, you amplify your ability to achieve, creating a ripple effect that extends far beyond your initial effort.

Audacious moves require a strong foundation, and that foundation is you. When you invest in yourself, you create the capacity to dream bigger, act braver, and live more fully. By choosing to fill your cup, you equip yourself to pour generously into everything that matters most—your career, your relationships, and your dreams. It's not just about the big decisions like hiring help; it's about cultivating habits and practices that fortify your well-being every day. Whether it's prioritizing sleep, fueling your body with nutritious food, exercising regularly, meditating, or seeking therapy, these investments pay dividends in your ability to tackle life's challenges and seize bold opportunities.

By now, you've heard how I was able to launch a media company, a clothing line, national events, and more, and if you're wondering how I do it all on a practical, daily level, I'm about to show you.

In this chapter, I'll share exactly how I've built a life that allows me to move audaciously. I'll take you behind the scenes and share the secrets to how I do what I do, and more importantly, I'll tell you the reasons why personal investment is the cornerstone of achieving success in every sphere. You'll learn the practices, habits, and mindset shifts that have been my foundation. Together, we'll explore how personal investment isn't just self-care; it's a strategy for sustainable success. Because when you invest in yourself, you create the conditions for your best

> **Personal investment is the cornerstone of transformation.**

The ROI of Investing in Yourself

life—and the audacious goals you've been dreaming of become entirely within reach. Are you ready to step into it? Let's go.

How I Learned to Invest in Myself

When I found out I was pregnant with twins, my initial reaction was fear. Self-doubt crept in, whispering that I couldn't possibly run a business and mother three kids at the same time. Well-meaning friends added fuel to that narrative, cautioning me to prepare for sacrifices and compromises. I began to internalize that story—the belief that I couldn't have it all. I worried that I would have to choose between being a present, invested mother and a successful entrepreneur.

But then, a pivotal moment changed everything. I realized I was holding on to a limiting story that wasn't even my own. I had accepted the narrative that motherhood and career success were mutually exclusive. That realization sparked a shift in my mindset: What if I chose to believe a different story?

The breakthrough came during a conversation with a friend who was preparing for her first baby. She mentioned hiring a night nurse—someone to help her care for her newborn so she could get the rest she needed and maintain balance. The idea struck me like lightning. Here was a woman investing in her well-being, understanding that her physical and emotional health were not negotiable. Her example exposed me to a new possibility: What if I, too, made my well-being a priority? What if I invested in myself?

That simple conversation became a turning point. I reached out to her for the contact information of the agency she used and began exploring the option. When I saw the cost, I hesitated. Hiring a night nurse seven nights a week for five and a half months was no small expense. It would be a hefty financial cost. But deep down, I knew this wasn't just a financial decision—it was an investment in my ability to thrive.

And so, I said "yes." Yes to getting the rest I needed. Yes to showing up as the best version of myself for my family and my business. Yes to creating space for overflow in my life. That investment transformed everything. With the help of the night nurse, I was able to maintain my physical health, nurture my mental clarity, and preserve my emotional peace during one of the most demanding seasons of my life. Not only did I thrive, but the rest of my family did as well.

This experience taught me an invaluable lesson: **Personal investment is non-negotiable for achieving audacious goals.**

The ROI of Self-Investment

Investing in yourself isn't just about feeling better—it's about unlocking your fullest potential in every role you play. Whether you're an entrepreneur building a dream business, a corporate professional climbing the ladder, a volunteer making an impact, or the CEO of your home, prioritizing your personal growth transforms how you show up in every area of your life. Personal investment is a non-negotiable, whether you're hiring cleaning services to keep your home in order, ordering food delivery to save precious time, or enlisting a personal stylist to elevate your professional appearance. These are not mere conveniences—they are strategic decisions that allow you to focus your energy on what truly matters. A high-achieving individual understands that success is not just about working harder but also about working smarter. It's about recognizing that you cannot—and should not—do it all alone. **This mindset shifts the narrative** from guilt or indulgence to empowerment and efficiency, enabling you to build a life where excellence is sustainable, not just aspirational.

When you take care of yourself—physically, mentally, and emotionally—you gain a competitive edge. The benefits of personal investment extend far beyond your well-being; they directly enhance your energy, focus, confidence, and creativity.

The Strategy for Investing in Yourself: C.A.R.E. Framework

When I need to reassess the areas in which I may need to invest more time or energy, I use the C.A.R.E framework and focus on these four areas: **Confidence, Adaptability, Relationships, and Energy**. This helps equip me to thrive, no matter the challenges or opportunities I face, and I know it will do the same for you!

C—Audacious Confidence
Confidence is the cornerstone of growth. It's not something you wait to feel—it's something you build through intentional action. By nurturing your self-worth, you project strength, clarity, and belief in your abilities, which inspires others to trust and follow you.
Practice: Regularly set and achieve small, meaningful goals.
How It Helps: Breaking down big ambitions into smaller wins reinforces your self-belief, builds momentum, and helps you see your capability in action.

Actionable Steps:

1. Set one to two mini goals each week that align with your big-picture aspirations.

2. Reflect daily on your accomplishments to celebrate progress and build gratitude.
3. Step outside your comfort zone frequently to challenge and grow your confidence muscles.

A—Audacious Adaptability

In a world of constant change, adaptability is your superpower. Investing in personal growth strengthens your ability to pivot, overcome setbacks, and seize new opportunities with grace and determination.

Practice: Engage in mindfulness and stress-management techniques.

How It Helps: Staying present and managing emotions equips you to handle surprises with resilience and clarity.

Actionable Steps:

1. Dedicate ten minutes daily to mindfulness exercises, like meditation or deep breathing.
2. Reframe setbacks as growth opportunities by asking, "What can I learn from this?"
3. Visualize yourself thriving through challenges to build a proactive mindset.

R—Audacious Relationships

Your connections are a multiplier for success. When you prioritize your well-being, you show up better for others, fostering relationships built on trust, empathy, and collaboration. These bonds are crucial for unlocking opportunities and expanding your impact.

Practice: Prioritize active listening and empathetic communication.

How It Helps: Deep, meaningful connections enhance collaboration, trust, and long-term success.

Actionable Steps:

1. Practice active listening by summarizing what others say to show understanding.
2. Schedule regular time to nurture relationships, whether professionally or personally.
3. Express gratitude often—thank colleagues, clients, and loved ones for their support and contributions.

E—Audacious Energy

Energy is the fuel for everything you do. By taking care of your body and mind, you unlock the vitality needed to perform at your highest level. A well-nurtured body supports sharper focus, better decision-making, and greater resilience.

Practice: Build daily routines around movement, nutrition, and rest.

How It Helps: Balanced habits sustain your energy, enabling you to show up consistently as your best self.

Actionable Steps:

1. Commit to thirty minutes of movement daily, from yoga to walking or fitness classes.
2. Plan nutrient-dense meals to stabilize energy and focus throughout the day.

3. Establish a calming bedtime routine to ensure seven to nine hours of restorative sleep.

Why C.A.R.E. Matters

When you invest in **Confidence, Adaptability, Relationships, and Energy,** you produce a domino effect that touches every area of your life. This isn't just about improving yourself—it's about elevating your career, inspiring your community, and becoming a role model for growth.

The more you pour into yourself, the greater your capacity to contribute to the world around you. And it starts with you. Embrace the C.A.R.E. framework and commit to showing up for yourself with intention and audacity. The results will not only transform your life but also inspire others to reach for their full potential.

Your Next Step: Begin today. Pick one actionable step from each pillar and make it your priority. Your investment will unlock a life of purpose, power, and possibility.

Living Audaciously: Behind the Scenes of My Life

Let me take you behind the scenes of how I live audaciously in every area of my life. I'm not just here to share tips—I'm here to show you what it really looks like to juggle a life filled with big dreams, meaningful relationships, and the occasional chaos of raising three kids under the age of three. It's messy, it's beautiful, and most of all, it's intentional.

Let's be real, balance isn't some magical state of perfection—it's a moving target. Some days, I get it right. Other days, I feel like I'm barely holding it together. But what I've learned is that thriving in every area of life requires a commitment to showing up, adjusting when needed, and investing in what matters most. Let me share how I do it and how you can too.

How I Manage My Morning Routine—My Life's Sanity

I discovered that success isn't just about grand strategies or life-changing decisions. It's about the small, consistent actions I take every day. My morning routine became the cornerstone of my productivity and well-being, transforming how I approach each day.

Before I made these changes, my mornings were chaotic. I'd rush through tasks, skip breakfast, and start my day feeling frazzled. The negativity I absorbed from turning on the news often lingered, affecting my focus and energy. But once I adopted a structured morning routine, everything shifted. Here are five things I do to set myself up for success with my morning routine.

1. Audacious Preparation

- **The Night Before:** My routine actually begins the night before. I prepare my schedule, lay out my clothes, and organize my workspace. This simple act clears my mind and eliminates decision fatigue, allowing me to wake up feeling ready and focused.
- **Why It Works:** This preparation saves time and mental energy, giving me a sense of control as I start my day.

2. Audacious Early Mornings

- **Wake-Up Time:** I wake up thirty minutes earlier than I used to. This extra time is a gift to myself—time

to be intentional before the demands of the day take over.
- **Why It Works:** A quiet, unrushed morning helps me feel centered and calm, setting a positive tone for the day.

3. *Audacious Movement*

- **Exercise:** I incorporate at least fifteen to twenty minutes of movement into my morning. This could be yoga, a quick workout, or a brisk walk.
- **Why It Works:** Physical activity boosts my energy, sharpens my focus, and helps me approach challenges with a clear mind.

4. *Audacious Eating Habits*

- **Breakfast:** I make time for a nutritious breakfast—something simple but healthy, like oatmeal with fruit or eggs with avocado.
- **Why It Works:** Fueling my body in the morning improves my focus and mood, ensuring I have the stamina to tackle the day.

5. *Audacious Intentions*

- **Visualization and Gratitude:** I spend a few minutes setting my intentions for the day. I visualize my goals, reflect on what I'm grateful for, and repeat positive affirmations.

- **Why It Works:** This practice cultivates a winning mindset, helping me approach the day with clarity and confidence.

Why This Routine Works for Me

Investing in this routine has been transformative. By starting my day with purpose and care, I've experienced:

- **Clarity:** My thoughts are more focused, and I make better decisions.
- **Productivity:** I accomplish more with less stress.
- **Energy:** I feel vibrant and capable, no matter how full my schedule is.

This routine is more than a series of steps—it's a statement of self-worth. By prioritizing my mornings, I'm reinforcing the belief that I deserve to thrive. When I invest in myself, I signal to the world—and to myself—that I'm serious about my success. The morning routine is my non-negotiable, but there are other routines I like to incorporate into my life.

How I Manage My Time: Running Two Businesses and a Family

Life in my world is beautifully full—some might even call it chaotic. With three little ones, a husband, a dog, and two businesses to run, the days feel like they're bursting at the seams. There's no "perfect formula" for managing it all, but I've found a rhythm that works for me—most days. Here's a real peek into how I prioritize my time to keep everything (and myself) afloat.

What I Do: Time-Blocking for Clarity and Peace of Mind

My calendar is my lifeline. It's not just a list of meetings or deadlines—it's a tool I use to make sure everything that matters gets space in my day. Work tasks, family dinners, playtime with the kids, self-care, even moments of rest—they all get blocked into my schedule. Why? Because if it's not on the calendar, it's too easy to let it slip through the cracks.

For example, my mornings start early (I mean *early*) because that's the only time I can carve out for myself before the house wakes up. I use this quiet window to pray, read scripture, or write in my journal and move my body—it's my way of grounding myself before the day begins. Once the kids are up, the focus shifts to breakfast chaos, diaper changes, and getting everyone ready for the day. From there, it's a mix of client calls, work projects, and the ever-important midday breaks when I try to squeeze in a quick workout or at least step outside for fresh air.

Afternoons are all about multitasking—wrapping up business priorities while keeping an eye on the kids, maybe sneaking in a dance party or some coloring time when they need my attention. And evenings? That's sacred family time. We have dinner together, unwind, and make space for connection. Once the kids are asleep, I might tackle a few leftover tasks, but I also make it a point to wind down with my husband or just enjoy a quiet moment alone.

Is it always seamless? Absolutely not. Some days, the schedule goes out the window because someone's sick, a meeting runs late, or life just *happens*. But having a plan in place gives me a foundation to fall back on, even when things get messy.

The lesson for you to apply to your life: Overcommitting leads to burnout, and that is why time-blocking allows you to stay focused. Commit to what's truly important by identifying your non-negotiables each day. Give yourself permission to say "no" to what doesn't serve your priorities. If it ain't on your calendar, it ain't real!

How I Nurture My Family: Creating Connection Amidst the Chaos

Family is my foundation, the heart of everything I do—but let's be real: With three little ones, a dog, and a husband, the chaos is nonstop. The dishes pile up, toys scatter across the floor, and some days, it feels like we're just running on fumes. But amidst all the mess, I've learned that connection doesn't have to be fancy or complicated—it just has to be intentional.

What I Do: Grounding Our Family in Simple Traditions
We've created fun, low-pressure traditions that help us connect. For example, Friday nights are for dance parties in the living room—the music goes up, and we laugh and twirl until we're out of breath. Afterward, we head to our favorite local cookie shop for a treat. It's a small thing, but it's become a ritual the kids look forward to all week. Those moments of laughter and sweetness remind us of what matters most.

Lesson for You: Presence over Perfection
Your family doesn't need perfection—they need *you*. It's not about orchestrating the "perfect" activity; it's about being

present and showing up consistently. Small, intentional traditions—like dance parties or a regular family outing—create a foundation of love and trust. The magic isn't in perfection; it's in the joy of simply being together.

How I Build a Thriving Marriage: Prioritizing Partnership

A strong marriage doesn't just happen—it's built through consistent, intentional effort. With the demands of kids, work, and everyday life, it would be easy to let our partnership drift into autopilot. But my husband and I have made a commitment to treat our relationship like the cornerstone it is—because when we're in sync, everything else runs more smoothly.

> Connection doesn't have to be fancy or complicated—it just has to be intentional.

What I Do: Performance Coaching and Radical Transparency
We approach our marriage like a dynamic team. Just like a car needs regular tune-ups, so do relationships. Every so often, we'll sit down and assess the state of our marriage—reviewing what's working, identifying areas for improvement, and aligning on our goals. It's not just about "fixing problems" but proactively creating the marriage we want.

To stay in sync, we also share everything on each other's calendars. It's not about micromanaging—it's about staying on the same page. Whether it's a work meeting, the kids' activities, or personal time, we know where the other person is and what's on their plate. This shared visibility fosters a sense of partnership and keeps communication flowing.

Lesson for You: Treat Your Marriage like a Partnership
Marriage thrives on intention and alignment. Regular check-ins—whether formal or informal—help you stay connected, share goals, and ensure you're working as a team. Radical transparency in communication, like sharing schedules or discussing dreams and challenges, creates trust and clarity. Don't let your marriage run on autopilot; nurture it like the meaningful partnership it is.

How I Manage Finances: Creating Stability and Peace

I'll be honest: I used to hate talking about money. It felt overwhelming, stressful, and like one more thing I'd rather avoid. But avoiding it didn't make the stress go away—in fact, it made it worse. Eventually, I realized that money is just numbers. It's not emotional unless we allow it to be. Once I pushed through the discomfort and shifted my mindset, I began to see money as a tool—a resource I could manage strategically rather than something that controlled me.

What I Do: Budgeting and Money Strategies
I've learned to approach money with a clear, proactive strategy. I use a budgeting app to track spending and automate savings so I always know where my money is going. Once a month, my husband and I have a "money meeting." It's not always fun (especially when things get tight), but it's crucial. We review our goals, adjust where needed, and celebrate small wins—like sticking to a budget or reaching a savings milestone. These meetings help us stay aligned and keep financial stress from building up. A study by Ramsey Solutions found that 87 percent of couples

who described their marriage as "great" also reported working together to set long-term financial goals. In contrast, only 41 percent of those who rated their marriage as "okay" or "in crisis" engaged in joint financial planning.

Lesson for You: Take Control, One Step at a Time
Talking about money doesn't have to be intimidating. Start by taking one small step—whether that's tracking your spending for a week, setting a tiny savings goal, or simply reviewing your finances without judgment. Progress, not perfection, is the goal. Money doesn't have to overtake you; by building strategies and staying consistent, you can create clarity, stability, and peace of mind in your financial life.

How I Cultivate Friendships: Staying Connected in Busy Seasons

Friendships are a lifeline, a source of joy and grounding—but let's be real: When life gets busy, it's easy for them to slip to the back burner. I've learned that maintaining strong connections doesn't require elaborate plans or hours of free time. Instead, it's about weaving small, meaningful efforts into my everyday life.

What I Do: Using Car Time to Connect
One of my favorite ways to stay in touch with friends is by using car time strategically. During school drop-offs and pick-ups, I'll often make calls to check in with friends. My kids hear these conversations, and it's a way for me to model that friendships matter and staying connected takes effort. Whether it's a quick chat or just leaving a voicemail, these moments help me nurture my relationships even during my busiest days.

On top of that, I set reminders to send a text, share a funny meme, or leave a voice note just to let someone know I'm thinking of them. And when I can, I love sneaking in a coffee date or planning a call—but even when I can't, the little things keep those friendships alive.

Lesson for You: Connection Doesn't Have to Be Big to Be Meaningful
Friendships aren't about how often you see or talk to someone—it's about showing up consistently, even in small ways. A quick call in the car, a thoughtful text, or sharing a laugh over a meme can go a long way. Don't wait for the perfect moment to reach out. Instead, use the time you already have to show your friends they matter. Little by little, those efforts build the kind of lasting, meaningful connections we all need.

Living audaciously isn't about getting it all perfect—it's about showing up for yourself and your priorities with intention. You don't have to follow my exact routines to thrive. The key is finding what works for *you*.

> Living audaciously isn't about getting it all perfect—it's about showing up for yourself and your priorities with intention.

An Audacious Life Requires Audacious Investment

Investing in yourself isn't optional—it's the price of admission to the life you truly deserve. It's not selfish; it's strategic. It's the foundation for achieving greatness, unlocking your full potential, and creating extraordinary results in every area of your life.

This isn't a one-time decision. It's a non-negotiable, lifelong commitment to growth. To sharpening your skills. To strengthening your mind and body. To aligning your actions with the vision you have for your future. Every effort, no matter how small, builds the foundation for your success and positions you to show up stronger, bolder, and more capable.

When you make yourself the priority, you're not just transforming your own life—you're sparking a movement. Your investment inspires others, deepens your relationships, and amplifies your impact in ways you can't yet imagine.

This is your moment. Decide now to make your growth and well-being your top priority. Pour into yourself unapologetically. Show up relentlessly. Because when you invest in yourself, there's no limit to what you can achieve.

> When you invest in yourself, there's no limit to what you can achieve.

It's time to bet on yourself. Start today.

CHAPTER 12

The Real Secret Sauce Is Surrender

NAKED IN FRONT OF the world. That's how I felt in one of the most humbling, vulnerable moments of my entrepreneurial journey. It wasn't the kind of nakedness that comes from public failure or harsh criticism; it was the raw exposure of my desperation, laid bare in front of someone I admired.

It began with a woman I had been following on Instagram. She was everything I wanted to be: confident, successful, magnetic. From the outside, she seemed to have unlocked the secrets to success that I was fumbling to grasp. When I saw that she was in Dallas for a fundraising event, my heart raced. This was it—my golden opportunity. Without hesitation, I slid into her DMs, nervously crafting a message introducing myself as a local entrepreneur and asking if we could meet.

To my amazement, she said yes. My excitement bordered on frenzy. I was certain this meeting would change everything. I envisioned a perfect conversation where she would see something special in me, take me under her wing, and hand me the keys to a new level of success. Fueled by hope and adrenaline, I threw on the most "professional" outfit I could find and drove an hour to meet her, rehearsing questions in my head the entire way.

When we sat down, I launched into my script. I asked about her journey, her strategies, her routines—anything that might reveal a hidden shortcut to success. My questions tumbled out one after another, each one betraying my hunger for answers, my longing for validation.

She listened patiently at first, nodding as I rattled off my queries. But then, after my third question, she stopped me. Her eyes locked onto mine, and in a calm but piercing voice, she said, "You sound desperate. Where are you leaving space for miracles?"

Her words landed like a punch to the gut. Shame prickled at the edges of my consciousness, and embarrassment flooded through me. I felt exposed, as if she had stripped away the carefully curated façade I had tried so hard to maintain. My throat tightened, and I fought the urge to defend myself, to explain that I wasn't desperate—I was just ambitious. But deep down, I knew she was right.

The truth I had been avoiding became glaringly clear at that moment: I was desperate. I was clinging so tightly to the idea that I could control my path to success that I had left no room for the unexpected, for grace, for the possibility that things could unfold in a way I hadn't planned. My relentless drive, my need to control every step, was suffocating the very magic I was searching for.

The Real Secret Sauce Is Surrender

Her words stayed with me long after that meeting. At first, they stung. I replayed the moment in my head, cringing at how frantic I must have sounded. But as the embarrassment faded, something deeper began to shift within me. I started to see that my desperation for control was rooted in fear—fear of failure, fear of not being enough. And in my attempt to avoid that fear, I had been blocking the flow of something far more powerful: surrender.

This moment became the foundation of a lesson I wish I had learned earlier: the tension between control and surrender. So many of us cling to the illusion that we can force our way to success, mapping out every step, executing every strategy with precision. But in doing so, we often overlook the transformative power of letting go. Surrender isn't about giving up; it's about creating space—space for miracles, for serendipity, for the kind of breakthroughs that only come when we loosen our grip and trust the process.

That woman's words didn't just shift my perspective; they cracked it wide open. I realized that surrendering doesn't mean abandoning ambition. It means finding the courage to stop clinging so tightly to the outcome and trusting that, sometimes, the very act of letting go is what accelerates our success.

This chapter is about that tension—the dance between control and surrender. It's about learning to recognize when your need to control is holding you back and finding the faith to loosen your grip. Because often, it's in the spaces we don't plan for, the gaps we don't fill, that miracles happen.

> **Often, it's in the spaces we don't plan for, the gaps we don't fill, that miracles happen.**

The Struggle of Surrender

The struggle of surrender lies in its paradoxical nature: How can letting go, a seeming act of passivity, lead to faster success? Surrender often feels like an admission of defeat, a relinquishing of control that leaves us vulnerable to chaos and failure. Yet true surrender is not about giving up; it's about releasing the obsessive need to control every outcome and trusting in a greater flow—one that we cannot always predict or manipulate.

Surrendering requires us to move beyond fear and embrace audacious faith: the bold belief that even in uncertainty, the unknown holds possibilities far greater than we can imagine. This kind of surrender demands courage because it goes against the grain of logic and societal expectations. It takes audacity to relinquish control and trust that the right opportunities, insights, and solutions will unfold—not through force, but through alignment and trust in the process. Far from being passive, surrender is an act of profound faith and bravery, allowing us to step into a flow that accelerates success in ways we could never engineer on our own.

The Myth of Control: Why We Cling to the Illusion

The myth of control is deeply ingrained in us. We cling to the illusion of control because it gives us the false sense of security that we can shape our outcomes, avoid failure, and protect ourselves from uncertainty. Control feels like a shield against chaos, a way to prove our competence and worthiness. Yet, this illusion comes with limitations. The need for control often traps us in rigid thinking, leaving little room for creativity, adaptability, or the unexpected opportunities that life presents. It drains our energy as we strive to manage every variable, only to find that outcomes often remain beyond our grasp. The harder we hold on, the more we realize how fragile and futile this approach can be.

This is where the need for surrender becomes apparent—not as a retreat, but as a conscious choice to release the burden of control. By surrendering, we open ourselves to new possibilities, trusting that the unknown can hold solutions and paths far greater than what our limited control could achieve.

> **Far from being passive, surrender is an act of profound faith and bravery, allowing us to step into a flow that accelerates success in ways we could never engineer on our own.**

Releasing What You Can't Control

We all carry invisible baggage—stories, situations, and emotions that weigh us down, often without realizing it. These are things we can't control, things we wish we could change but can't. And the longer we hold on to them, the heavier they become, draining our energy and stealing our joy.

But what if freedom lies in letting go? What if the magic happens when we release what we can't control and give ourselves permission to stop carrying that weight?

The first step is acknowledgment. It's natural to want to fix things, especially when we care deeply. But fighting the uncontrollable only traps us in frustration. Accepting what's beyond our power isn't giving up—it's wisdom. It allows us to focus on what we *can* control: our actions, our responses, and our attitudes.

This shift is liberating. When we stop wasting energy on the unchangeable, we reclaim it for what truly matters: our growth, our happiness, and our peace of mind. Letting go empowers us—it's a declaration that we are in charge of how we navigate life's twists and turns.

> **When we stop wasting energy on the unchangeable, we reclaim it for what truly matters: our growth, our happiness, and our peace of mind.**

Of course, it's not always easy. There will be moments when life feels overwhelming. But each time we release the burden of what we can't control, we step closer to peace, authenticity, and purpose. The journey ahead is ours to shape, and the power to do so begins with letting go.

What Surrender Is and Isn't: Clearing Up Misconceptions

Surrender is often misunderstood, conjuring images of giving up or losing control. But true surrender is far from passive or defeatist—it's a powerful act of faith and trust. To fully embrace surrender, it's important to understand what it is and what it isn't.

What Surrender Is:

- **Surrender is an active decision to trust.** Surrender means intentionally releasing your tight grip on control and placing your trust in a force greater than yourself. It's a conscious choice to believe that life, God, or the universe is working in your favor, even when you can't see the full picture.
- **Surrender is aligning with flow.** It's not about stepping back from effort or ambition; it's about stepping into alignment. Surrender allows you to stop

The Real Secret Sauce Is Surrender

resisting the natural flow of events and start working *with* the currents of life instead of against them.
- **Surrender is creating space for miracles.** By letting go of the need to control every detail, you make room for unexpected breakthroughs and opportunities. Surrender invites serendipity, grace, and solutions that may not have been part of your original plan but are exactly what you need.

What Surrender Isn't:

- **Surrender is not an act of resignation.** Surrender doesn't mean buying into the notion of "whatever will be will be." No. Surrender is an *active*, courageous choice to release control and *actively* create space for something greater than yourself to work in your life.
- **Surrender isn't giving up.** Letting go doesn't mean abandoning your dreams or goals. Surrender is about holding on to your vision with faith while releasing your need to dictate exactly how and when it will come to fruition.
- **Surrender isn't passivity.** It's not about sitting idly by and waiting for things to happen. Surrender requires taking inspired action, but it also means trusting that the results will unfold in their own time and way.
- **Surrender isn't a lack of ambition.** Choosing to surrender doesn't mean you stop striving or dreaming

big. It means that your ambition is tempered with trust, allowing you to pursue your goals without becoming consumed by anxiety or fear.

Surrender is not about letting go of your dreams—it's about trusting the path to achieving them, even when it looks different from what you initially imagined. When you surrender, you open yourself to new possibilities and unexpected opportunities that you couldn't have planned for. You allow life to work its magic, connecting you to people, resources, and ideas that align with your purpose.

In fact, surrender can enhance your pursuit of your dreams. When you release the pressure to control every outcome, you free up energy and creativity. You become more open to trying new approaches, pivoting when needed, and seeing potential where you once saw obstacles. Surrender doesn't diminish your dream—it expands the way you approach it, making room for a journey that's not only successful but also fulfilling and aligned with who you are meant to become.

> **Surrender is not about letting go of your dreams—it's about trusting the path to achieving them, even when it looks different from what you initially imagined.**

By redefining surrender in this way, you can begin to see it not as a limitation but as a profound tool for growth, transformation, and success.

The Benefits of Surrender

Surrender is an invitation for grace, intuition, and serendipity to guide you in ways your planning never could. By choosing surrender, you unlock the potential for miracles—those unforeseen breakthroughs and opportunities that can propel you toward your audacious goals with unexpected speed and ease. In fact, the benefits of surrender are more profound than you might realize. Surrender...

- Frees your energy from the exhausting grip of control
- Fosters clarity by allowing your intuition to surface
- Invites collaboration with forces beyond your understanding, whether you call it God, the universe, or divine timing
- Cultivates resilience, helping you adapt to change with grace
- Nurtures trust in the process, reducing the anxiety that comes with constant striving

When you surrender, you don't lose power—you shift it, tapping into a flow that accelerates your journey in ways you couldn't have orchestrated on your own. Let me share with you a remarkable story of how I saw surrender—that simple act of letting go—accelerate the blessings on my journey.

My Miracle in the Making: When Surrender Unlocked a Blessing

It was the end of the year, and the pressure was suffocating. Unexpected expenses had accumulated, and the numbers simply didn't add up. The funds to pay my employees—the people who had dedicated their time and energy to growing this dream alongside me—just weren't there. I felt the panic rising like a tidal wave, threatening to drown me. My mind raced with frantic thoughts: *How am I going to make this work? How did I let it get to this point?*

Audacious

For hours, I wrestled with the problem, searching for a solution that didn't exist. But then, something within me shifted. Exhausted and emotionally spent, I sat still, closed my eyes, and released it all. *God, I don't know how, but I trust You.* It wasn't easy—surrender never is—but in that moment, I chose to believe that even though I couldn't see a way forward, one existed. I let go, handed over my fears, and surrendered the outcome.

That was when the miracle happened. The very next day, my phone rang. It was a representative from a sponsor I had worked with the year prior, someone I hadn't spoken to in months. Their tone was warm, almost excited, as they explained that their organization had $100,000 left in their budget for the year. They wanted to allocate it to my business to make an impact in any way I saw fit.

I was stunned. Tears welled up in my eyes as I listened to them talk. It felt surreal, like a direct confirmation that surrender wasn't just a practice—it was the bridge between my faith and the blessings waiting to be unlocked. The money came at exactly the right time, covering payroll and leaving room for the initiatives that would take us into the new year stronger than ever.

I couldn't deny the connection between my surrender and the miraculous outcome. Letting go had made room for something greater than I could have imagined—a blessing I hadn't orchestrated or earned through control, but one I had received through trust and faith.

Now, the concept of surrender might be a new one for you, or one you find challenging if you struggle with the concept of believing in something greater than yourself or have never considered a relationship with God. I had the benefit of growing up in a family with deep spiritual roots. However, it wasn't until I was seven that I knew for myself that there was someone much bigger than me that was divinely orchestrating my life.

Let me tell you where my journey with God and faith all started, because that's where my belief in the power of miracles began.

My Journey to Faith: The Origin of My Trust

At just seven years old, I gave my life to Christ. Looking back, I didn't fully understand the weight of that decision, but there was something in me that knew it was important. Faith wasn't just a part of my life—it was woven into the very fabric of my being. Growing up with my grandmother, who was the church secretary, church wasn't a place we visited on Sundays—it was the heartbeat of our community. The small congregation we were part of might not have been large by worldly standards—maybe 150 people on a good Sunday—but it was thriving in spirit, and that was all that mattered.

I can still remember that day so clearly. I went to church with my aunt and cousin, and as we pulled into the gravel parking lot, that humble white building came into view. Simple, unassuming, but with a cross at the center that somehow made it feel like holy ground. The moment I stepped out of the car, I could hear the sound of the organ, the rhythm of hands clapping in unison. It was like the whole building was alive, swaying with the spirit. We slid into the second-to-last pew, and I sat there on the edge, my feet barely touching the floor.

Two and a half hours later, the preacher extended the invitation: "Come, join the church, give your life to Christ." The choir sang, "We offer Christ to you, oh my brother, oh my sister," and I felt something I couldn't fully explain. It was more than music—it was the presence of the Holy Spirit, powerful and overwhelming. Then, without even thinking, I stood up. I followed my aunt and cousin to the front, my body trembling, but I felt the energy of the room—of the people, of the choir, of the Holy Spirit—lifting me. I was just seven, but in that moment, everything changed. I began a relationship with God that would carry me through the highs and lows of life. From that day on, my faith would grow, being shaped by the church, by the community, and by the many lessons—both uplifting and challenging—that would come along the way. Believing in something bigger than myself and making space for miracles would prove to be a core theme throughout my life.

Surrendering My Dreams

At the age of seventeen years old, I received my first "real" Bible, the *Woman, Thou Art Loosed* Bible by the renowned T. D. Jakes, and it quickly became more than a sacred book—it became the blueprint for my life.

In the back of that Bible, I began to write down the vision for my future. I wrote with boldness and clarity, pouring my hopes and dreams onto the pages. I listed the scholarships I wanted to win, the car I dreamed of driving to college, the schools I hoped to attend, and the major I planned to pursue. Alongside these dreams, I wrote my guiding scripture: Jeremiah 29:11—*"For I know the plans I have for you, declares the Lord, plans to prosper you and not to harm you, plans to give you hope and a future."*

At the time, I didn't fully understand the magnitude of what I was doing. To me, it felt like a simple act of faith—putting pen

The Real Secret Sauce Is Surrender

to paper and trusting that God was listening. But looking back now, I realize it was the first step in surrendering my dreams to something greater. It wasn't just about setting goals; it was about aligning those goals with God's plan for my life and trusting that He would bring them to fruition.

Over time, I watched in awe as everything I wrote down began to manifest. The scholarships came through, the acceptance letters arrived, and even the car I had dreamed of was parked in my driveway. But it didn't stop there. What truly amazed me were the things I couldn't have anticipated—the unexpected lessons I learned through struggles, the doors that opened when others closed, and the profound growth that came from trusting in God's plan.

Later I looked back and realized this was the blueprint for surrender: to write your vision, to believe in something bigger than yourself, and to release control of the *how* and *when.*

Here's what I've come to understand: Surrender isn't about sitting back and doing nothing; it's about taking inspired action while trusting that God will handle the rest. It's about believing that His plans for you are bigger and better than anything you could imagine for yourself.

Looking back, I see how that simple act of writing in the back of my Bible wasn't just an exercise in goal-setting—it was an act of faith. It was my way of saying, *God, I trust You to take these dreams and make them real in Your time and in Your way.* And He did, exceeding my expectations in ways I never thought possible.

This is the power of surrender: to believe in something greater, to trust in God's promises, and to let go of control so that miracles can unfold. And it all starts with faith—the kind that is audacious enough to dream and humble enough to surrender.

> Surrender isn't about sitting back and doing nothing; it's about taking inspired action while trusting that God will handle the rest.

With this understanding of surrender, we now turn to practical steps you can take to embrace this transformative mindset in your own life.

How to Surrender

Surrender is not a single moment of letting go—it's a practice, a mindset that requires continual effort and intention. It's a journey of releasing control and stepping into trust, one decision at a time. Here's how to begin to shift into this mentality:

1. **Acknowledge Your Struggle.** The first step to surrender is awareness. Take an honest look at your life and identify where you're clinging to control. Where are you forcing things to happen, holding on too tightly to specific outcomes, or resisting the natural flow of events? Acknowledging these areas is not a sign of failure but a powerful act of self-awareness. It's how you begin to shift your mindset.
2. **Release Attachment to the Outcome.** Pursue your goals with intention and effort, but hold them lightly. Release the need for things to unfold in a specific way or according to a rigid timeline. Trust that life—or God, or the universe—knows what is best for you and will deliver it in the right way and time. Detaching from the outcome frees you to stay open to possibilities you might not have envisioned.
3. **Practice Daily Trust.** Surrender is a daily practice, not an all-or-nothing event. Each day, make the

The Real Secret Sauce Is Surrender

conscious choice to trust: Trust yourself, trust the process, and trust that you're being guided, even when the path is unclear. Start small. Choose one area of your life where you can let go and observe the results. With time, you'll strengthen your ability to surrender in bigger, more meaningful ways.

4. **Let Go of the "How."** You don't need to figure out every step or detail of how your goals will be achieved. Focus on what you desire—what you want to create, feel, or achieve—and let life handle the "how." When you micromanage the process, you limit the ways in which solutions and opportunities can present themselves. By letting go of the "how," you invite creativity and unexpected breakthroughs into your journey.

5. **Stay Present.** Surrender requires grounding yourself in the present moment. It's easy to dwell on past mistakes or worry about future uncertainties, but neither is where surrender takes place. True surrender happens in the here and now—when you trust that this moment, just as it is, is enough and that each step will reveal itself in time.

Surrender is an active and intentional practice, one that requires patience and faith. By following these steps, you'll begin to open yourself to a life in which miracles, unexpected opportunities, and effortless flow can unfold.

Once you shift into a mindset of surrender, there are some spiritual habits that can help you deepen your faith. These are habits I've practiced from a young age that have become sweeter and more precious to me with each passing year. Audacious vision takes audacious faith, and I couldn't have achieved all that I did without these spiritual habits to keep me encouraged in the valleys and levelheaded on the mountains. These habits have the power to transform your dreams from ceaseless striving into beautiful surrender and satisfaction.

Spiritual Habits to Deepen Your Faith

Faith isn't just a belief—it's a living, breathing practice. Through intentional spiritual habits, we create a foundation that deepens our relationship with God and aligns our lives with His purpose. Below are strategies for cultivating these habits in your daily life.

Strategy #1: Develop a Morning Prayer Habit

The Power of Prayer

Prayer is a habit I rely on daily—sometimes even multiple times a day. It's more than a routine; it's a lifeline, a powerful practice that connects me to something greater than myself. You might be thinking, *I've heard this before,* or *I'm not a spiritual person—how does this apply to me?* But prayer, no matter your belief system, has the potential to be a transformative force in your life.

For me, prayer is where I release my fears, surrender what I can't control, and find the strength to keep moving forward. It's a moment of humility and trust—a way of acknowledging that while I don't have all the answers, I believe in a higher purpose guiding my path. Prayer also creates space for transformation. It's a practice of surrender, releasing the need for control and embracing trust. When you let go of trying to manage every

The Real Secret Sauce Is Surrender

outcome, you invite peace into your life. You start to recognize synchronicities—those moments when things unexpectedly align, people show up at the right time, or opportunities unfold in ways you couldn't have planned.

The real power of prayer lies in surrender. It's not just about asking for what you want; it's about releasing your grip on life's uncertainties and trusting that you are being guided. When you pray with intention and let go of control, you create space for miracles to unfold. You remind yourself that you are supported, worthy, and capable of navigating anything life throws your way.

Now, I'm not a pastor, but I can tell you this from my heart: I've placed many things on the prayer table, and time and time again, God has shown up for me in ways I couldn't have imagined. I believe He will do the same for you. Your journey of prayer is not just about asking for things—it's about audaciously making the investment in yourself, opening up space for growth, and trusting that the divine will guide you every step of the way.

Go ahead, friend—it's your time. God is with you every step of the way. Here's how you can start this habit. Every morning, begin your day with intentional prayer. Find a quiet space, even if it's just five minutes, and start by thanking God for the gift of life and the blessings in your life. Use this time to express gratitude for His guidance, surrender your worries, and ask for His wisdom to navigate the day ahead.

A simple structure for your prayer can look like this:

1. Praise: Acknowledge God's greatness and faithfulness. *Example*: "Lord, thank You for Your unwavering love and the blessings You pour into my life."

2. Surrender: Share your challenges and invite Him into every area of your day.
   Example: "God, I give You my plans and my worries today. Let Your will guide me in every decision."
3. Gratitude: Name specific things you are grateful for.
   Example: "Thank You for my family, my health, and the opportunities You've placed before me."

As this becomes a daily habit, you'll notice how prayer shifts your mindset from worry to trust and anchors you in God's peace before the day unfolds.

Strategy #2: Immerse Yourself in Daily Devotional Reading
Carve out time each day, preferably in the morning, to dive into a devotional or scripture passage. Choose devotionals that align with your current season of life—whether you're seeking guidance, strength, or hope. Pair this with intentional journaling to reflect on what you've read and how it applies to your life.

To stay consistent, keep your materials accessible—a Bible, devotional book, or Bible app on your phone. Here's a framework to deepen your reading:

1. Pray Before You Read: Ask the Holy Spirit for understanding and clarity.
   Example: "Lord, speak to me through Your word and reveal what I need to hear today."

2. Reflect on the Message: What stood out to you in the passage? Is there a specific call to action or reassurance you needed?
3. Apply It: Identify one way you can incorporate the wisdom into your actions today.
    Example: If you read about trust, focus on letting go of a specific worry and relying on God's timing.

Over time, this habit will build a reservoir of wisdom that you can draw from in moments of challenge or decision-making.

Strategy #3: Stand on Scriptures
In moments of doubt, fear, or uncertainty, standing on God's promises through scripture is a powerful way to remain anchored. Identify key verses that resonate with your journey and commit them to memory. Use them as affirmations to speak life and faith into your situation.

Here are a few audacious scriptures to incorporate into your life:

- Joshua 1:9: *Be strong and courageous. Do not be afraid; do not be discouraged, for the Lord your God will be with you wherever you go.*
    Apply it: When faced with fear or self-doubt, recite this verse to remind yourself of God's constant presence.

- Jeremiah 29:11: *"For I know the plans I have for you,"* declares the Lord, *"plans to prosper you and not to harm you, plans to give you hope and a future."*
    Apply it: When you feel uncertain about the future, use this scripture as a declaration of trust in God's plans.

- Philippians 4:13: *I can do all things through Christ who strengthens me.*
    Apply it: Use this verse to push through challenges, knowing that God equips you with the strength you need.

Standing on scripture equips you to face life boldly, knowing that His word never fails.

Strategy #4: Cultivate Community Worship and Fellowship
Faith flourishes in community. Make it a priority to connect with others who share your values through church, small groups, or other faith-based gatherings. Weekly worship provides a space to recharge spiritually, hear God's word, and find encouragement from others walking similar paths.

Here's how to deepen this habit:

1. Find Your Space: Whether it's a local church, a virtual Bible study, or a prayer group, choose a setting that aligns with your faith journey.
2. Engage Fully: Don't just show up—participate! Serve in a ministry, volunteer, or join a group discussion.

The Real Secret Sauce Is Surrender

This active involvement strengthens your sense of belonging and purpose.
3. Extend Fellowship Beyond Sunday: Schedule coffee chats, meals, or calls with members of your faith community. These relationships are a source of encouragement and accountability.

Through community worship, you'll not only feel supported but also inspire others through your presence and testimony.

Strategy #5: Practice Gratitude Daily
Gratitude is a spiritual practice that transforms your perspective. Begin and end each day by reflecting on the blessings in your life. Create a gratitude journal where you list three things you're thankful for each day. They can be as big as a career breakthrough or as simple as a kind word from a friend.

Here's how to build a habit of gratitude:

1. Anchor It to Daily Routines: Pair your gratitude practice with an existing habit, like morning coffee or evening wind-down time.
2. Be Specific: Instead of general statements like "I'm grateful for my health," note something specific: "I'm grateful I had the energy to tackle a busy day."
3. Incorporate It into Prayer: Start your prayers with gratitude to keep your focus on God's blessings, even in challenging times.

Gratitude shifts your focus from what's missing to what's present, filling your heart with joy and contentment.

By cultivating these spiritual habits—morning prayer, devotional reading, standing on scripture, community worship, and gratitude—you'll deepen your faith and create a life anchored in purpose and peace. Let these practices guide your journey, reminding you that **faith isn't a passive belief but an active, transformative way of living.**

Embracing the Unknown and Unlocking Miracles

Living audaciously requires audacious faith—the kind of faith that allows you to let go of control and trust in the unknown. Surrender is the bridge between where you are and where you want to be, unlocking miracles and accelerating your journey toward your boldest goals. It's not about abandoning your dreams but about trusting that they can unfold in even greater ways than you imagined.

When you choose surrender, you invite grace, creativity, and divine timing into your life. You open yourself to breakthroughs that your own striving could never accomplish. My journey is proof of this truth, and now it's your turn. Take the leap of faith. Let go of the need to control every step, and watch how the process unfolds. The power of surrender is available to you too—and with it, you'll discover a life filled with purpose, miracles, and success beyond measure.

Be audacious. Dare to dream, even after heartbreak. Dare to act, even after failure. Dare to surrender, even when it feels like giving up. Your life is waiting for you—not the perfect version of you, but the real, messy, bold, and brilliant you.

Conclusion

AS YOU CLOSE THIS book, I want you to pause for a moment and truly take it all in. You've just spent hours investing in yourself, absorbing stories, lessons, and strategies. But let me be clear—reading this book, or any other book, won't change your life. The one thing standing between you and a transformed, purposeful, audacious life is *you*.
   You have to decide.
   Decide to take action. Decide to absorb the words you've read, not just as an inspiration but as a call to do something about your dreams. Decide to believe in yourself, even when it feels impossible. Because here's the truth: No one can make the decision for you. No one else will show up for your life the way you can. It's your moment, your chance, your time to be bold, to bet on yourself, and to create a life you're proud of.
   But there's one more thing. The real secret sauce—the game-changing, life-shifting truth I've discovered—is what I just shared with you in the last chapter: **surrender.**

Conclusion

I spent so much time striving, pushing, hustling, and trying to control every outcome. And while every piece of wisdom I've shared with you is important, my life only truly began to change for the better when I surrendered. For me, that surrender wasn't just about letting go—it was about trusting something greater than myself. It was about giving my plans, my fears, and my dreams to God and trusting that His purpose for me was bigger, better, and more fulfilling than anything I could imagine.

Surrender isn't giving up; it's giving in to a higher calling, a higher power, a greater purpose. It's the doorway to a life that's not just full of activity, but full of meaning.

Now I want you to win.

I want you to take everything you've read, all the lessons, all the inspiration, and go after your dreams with boldness. I want you to live boldly, love fiercely, and walk through life with the unshakable belief that you are capable of incredible things. You're here for a reason. You were created with a purpose, and the world is waiting for you to step into it.

The time for hesitation is over. This is your moment. Go live the audacious life you've always dreamed of. Dream big, act bigger, and don't let fear, doubt, or failure hold you back. The life you've been waiting for is already yours to claim—all you have to do is say yes.

Say yes to yourself. Say yes to the unknown. Say yes to surrender. And watch how everything changes.

Now go. Live boldly. Believe in yourself. And never, ever stop being *audacious*.

Acknowledgments

FIRST AND FOREMOST, THANK you, God. You knew the exact moment I was supposed to write this book—even when I didn't. You knew the lessons I had to live through so that those very lessons could one day become a light for someone else. Only You could have orchestrated the timing, the shaping, the stretching, the clarity. I'm so thankful that You continue to use me—not because I've done everything right, but because I've stayed available.

At forty years old, I now understand that true fulfillment is found in chasing what You desire for my life, not what the world says I should want. That has been the secret sauce—releasing what's not mine, resting in what is, and no longer forcing things that were never assigned to me in the first place.

This book is a reflection of that surrender. Of what it means to keep going, even when it doesn't make sense.

To my husband, Kevin, and my children, Elle, Laila, and Ryan—thank you for loving me through every version of myself. Every early morning, late night, school run, missed

Acknowledgments

school lunch and trading it for Uber Eats, or deadline—you have been my grounding force. Your patience and your presence made space for this dream to come alive. I hope one day, you'll read these words and feel just how loved you are.

To my tribe, my village, my people—thank you. You have clapped for me, covered me, reposted and rallied for me, poured into me when I was pouring out. Whether we've walked together for a decade or connected just recently, you've been part of the scaffolding that held me up as I built. I don't take it lightly. Your love has lifted me more times than I can count.

There are also those *assigned* to me—people God specifically placed in my path not by chance, but by divine design. Angie, you helped me rewrite my story and make it work for me, not against me. You have prayed for me, cried with me, and reminded me of my power when I was ready to give up on it. Shawntee, your constant encouragement and unwavering belief in me have been a gift I never even knew I needed. Thank you both for loving me out loud.

To Mattie James—thank you for opening the door to the publishing world by introducing me to my agent, Lisa. That simple act changed everything. To my agent—thank you for saying yes to me when all I had was a vision and a voice. And to my editor, Beth—thank you for seeing my story clearly, for holding space for my truth, and for helping me shape it into something honest, impactful, and lasting. Your belief in this book made me believe deeper in it too.

This isn't just a book—it's an offering. A love letter to audacity. A reminder to anyone reading that it's possible to live out what's been placed inside you. That what's ahead is worth the risk, worth the reach, worth the roar.

Thank you for walking with me. For believing in me. For being part of this holy, human, messy, miraculous journey.

About the Author

DALLAS-BASED ENTREPRENEUR and designer Marty McDonald left her career in corporate America to launch her first company, Boss Women Media, in 2017. Implementing her business savvy from years of partnerships with various Fortune 100 companies, Marty took an idea for connecting ambitious women and turned Boss Women Media into not just a company, but a movement—including the multi-city *Black Girl Magic Tour*, the annual Boss Woman of the Year Summit, and a loyal membership community of over two hundred thousand women. Because Marty knows many women allow fear to hold them back from accomplishing their goals, she founded Boss Women Media with a mission to help women achieve more and remove fear as the barrier to their big goals and dreams.

In addition to Boss Women Media, Marty also runs a successful children's wear company, Elle Olivia. Marty was inspired to create this brand after her daughter, Elle, was born in 2021 with a congenital diaphragmatic hernia, which meant she would need immediate surgery and a thirty-five-day NICU

About the Author

stay afterward to heal. During that time, Marty quickly realized her daughter would need two key things to navigate the world: advocacy and representation. From this realization, Marty and her husband dedicated their energies to addressing some systemic issues Black parents face, such as representation in children's clothing. The Elle Olivia brand is dedicated to showing girls big possibilities through the clothes they wear. Since its launch in 2022, the Elle Olivia brand has been carried in over four hundred Target locations nationwide. Marty lives in Dallas with her husband, Kevin, her daughter, Elle Olivia, and her twin son and daughter, Ryan and Laila. Marty enjoys spending time with family and friends, all while building the future of her dreams!

RAISING READERS
Books Build Bright Futures

Thank you for reading this book and for being a reader of books in general. As an author, I am so grateful to share being part of a community of readers with you, and I hope you will join me in passing our love of books on to the next generation of readers.

Did you know that reading for enjoyment is the single biggest predictor of a child's future happiness and success?

More than family circumstances, parents' educational background, or income, reading impacts a child's future academic performance, emotional well-being, communication skills, economic security, ambition, and happiness.

Studies show that kids reading for enjoyment in the US is in rapid decline:

- In 2012, 53% of 9-year-olds read almost every day. Just 10 years later, in 2022, the number had fallen to 39%.
- In 2012, 27% of 13-year-olds read for fun daily. By 2023, that number was just 14%.

Together, we can commit to **Raising Readers** and change this trend. How?

- Read to children in your life daily.
- Model reading as a fun activity.
- Reduce screen time.
- Start a family, school, or community book club.
- Visit bookstores and libraries regularly.
- Listen to audiobooks.
- Read the book before you see the movie.
- Encourage your child to read aloud to a pet or stuffed animal.
- Give books as gifts.
- Donate books to families and communities in need.

Books build bright futures, and **Raising Readers** is our shared responsibility.

For more information, visit **JoinRaisingReaders.com**

Sources: National Endowment for the Arts, National Assessment of Educational Progress, WorldBookDay.org, Nielsen BookData's 2023 "Understanding the Children's Book Consumer"